'The Re-Vision therapy program in Londo
world, showing us new and profound ways
ual and social. This book is a roadmap for th
up by many professions. I will read it again a
stunning complexity as I help others find th
—**Thomas Moore**,
Author of *Care of the Soul*

'In the last few years I have had the opportunity to be a guest lecturer at Re-Vision where I saw in practice the excellent and important work that Re-Vision
began thirty years ago. That work is now even more necessary as our political,
economic, educational and medical institutions are collapsing and ecological
crises are threatening the very real possibility of environmental disaster. *Transformation in Troubled Times* speaks in a clear voice, summoning therapists, ed-
ucators, environmentalists, psychologists and all concerned citizens to be
responsive to our current crises'.
—**Robert D. Romanyshyn**, Ph.D.,
Author of *The Wounded Researcher: Research with Soul in Mind*,
Emeritus Professor of Clinical Psychology and Affiliate Member of
The Inter-Regional Society of Jungian Analysts.

'Beyond the lands of psychotherapeutic diagnostics and techniques is a field
that Re-Vision, through the innovative work that Chris and Ewa Robertson
began, has inhabited for many years – it is the place where our wounded humanity and soulful longing is welcomed and heard.

'In this thoughtful and wise book, the authors invite us to listen with a more
poetic ear to deep stories of suffering and joy. Indeed, in the chaos of these troubling times, there has never been a greater need for this work as we search for
freedom, meaning and healing.

'Throughout the years, I have always been impressed with Re-Vision grad-
uates. They have a capacity to listen with deep presence and offer clarity of vi-
sion and understanding on what healing means in the 21st century. We get a
glimpse of that vision (and of the training) as each contributor articulates the
fundamental ground of psychotherapeutic skilful action and thought that Re-
Vision has carefully crafted. Its wisdom is both fresh and ancient.'
—**Dr Jan Jian Mojsa,**
UKCP Registered Psychotherapist & Supervisor,
Buddhist Chaplain,
Visiting Fellow, School of Health and Social Care, Bournemouth University

Transformation in Troubled Times

Re-Vision's Soulful Approach to Therapeutic Work

Compiled and edited by

Chris Robertson & Sarah Van Gogh

TransPersonal
Press

TransPersonal Press
(*a Kaminn Media imprint*)
Delft Cottage, Dyke
Forres IV36 2TF
Scotland
transpersonalpress.com

A CIP record for this title is available from the British Library.

ISBN 978-1-912698-02-8 (print)
ISBN 978-1-912698-03-5 (ebook)

Cover illustration *Igniculus* by Julie Harding
Page 6 Illustration *Colony Collapse* by Una d'Aragona
Edited by Kathleen White (intheworkscoaching.com)
Cover and text design and layout by Thierry Bogliolo

Printed, bound and distributed by Ingram Spark

Contents

With heartfelt thanks to the Re-Vision community

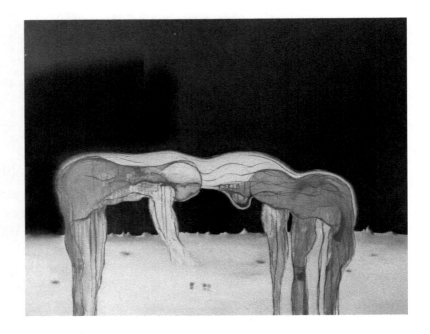

List of Illustrations

Introduction

By removing the soul from the world and not recognizing that the soul is also *in* the world, psychotherapy can't do its job anymore. The buildings are sick, the institutions are sick, the banking system's sick, the schools, the streets—the sickness is out *there*. —James Hillman[1]

There are calls in our present dark times not to lose heart, not to despair. There are calls for new heroes to fight new wars to save our species and planet. We will take a different tack, a re-visioning which offers a fresh perspective through which to see our world and its troubles. While not treating these troubles as delusions, which we can somehow ignore, the old solutions of finding a hero to save us might be missing a complex context.

Over its thirty-year history, Re-Vision has evolved its own unique perspective that draws from transpersonal, systemic, gestalt and psychodynamic traditions. From its onset, it been interested in the collective – that larger psyche beyond the place we commonly regard as 'mine'. As our culture's crisis deepens, many of its issues appear in the consulting room masquerading as personal. Even when recognized as trans-personal, the question is: How to engage with these deep issues in a way that is psychological rather than a style of social work?

The majority of a civilization in decline simply doesn't want to hear the truth about the situation because the future seems too bleak. Medicine has become a business where the dividend competes with client needs. Religious life is gripped with disclosures about abuse. Consuming is the new worship. The technological triumph over nature has the consequence of poisoning our environment, air, water and food. Denial is rife: denial of sexual abuse, denial of climate change, denial of racism. How can we bear it?

There is plenty to be depressed about as we look around in our world. The parallel between personal and collective troubles shifts the context away from individual salvation towards a sense of engagement with and compassion for the terrible losses being suffered. The work in the consulting room can be part of a bigger enterprise. In order for such work not to be an overly masochistic exercise, there needs to be a reason to do it – the *telos* of 'for what?' The willingness to bear with our wounds opens our eyes and potentially our hearts to what is going on around us. A wounded planet is also potentially a healing planet.

This close affinity between wounding and healing is central to Re-Vision's ethos. As Chapter 2 on the wounded healer elucidates, it takes work to turn the affliction of wounding into a healing potential. Much of this work involves acknowledgement of the pain and acceptance of the necessary difficulties and gifts that have helped shape life.

When Re-Vision started there was little acknowledgement of shadow in transpersonal therapy other than in the Jungian tradition. Through persistently naming and working with shadow issues, both in the consulting room and the organization, the Re-Vision culture is sensitized to shadow's ongoing appearance. Perhaps through facing into the shadow, the collective stain of the human condition and its toxic residue can be given a place. Such acceptance might be the remedy for a dark age: to learn to see in the dark, to be at peace in the dark, and to have, as Rainer Maria Rilke says in his poem, 'You darkness, that I come from... I have faith in nights'.[2]

To restore our faith in nights requires a remedy for mistrust of the dark and the failure to listen to our soul. We need to 'unforget' (anamnesis) old language and old stories that tell us why we should not turn our back on suffering (our own, other people's, other beings', the world's), but rather look into the suffering and bear with it, which is what love allows. Something of these stories is told in this book.

We describe Re-Vision's roots and its difference – its attempts not to perpetuate the dominant ego psychologies of adjustment, and how it has attempted to recognize the troubled waters of our time and fashion a transformational craft to travel through them.

In the following chapters, you will find different voices and ideas from within the Re-Vision training team, and also some common threads and themes which are fundamental to a soulful approach to the therapeutic work we practise and teach. One of those central themes is the importance of descending to the depths, and the need to include and attend to the dark, to shadow, to mystery and difficulty.

The opening chapter reaches back in time to its origins, the dreams which dreamt Re-Vision into existence. As Jo-Ann Roden suggests in Chapter 7 on the Re-Vision method, the early seeds of a system hold a template for what emerges. Ewa and Chris Robertson's faith in this original inspiration carried them through the inevitable trials and tribulations of starting afresh by seeing with new eyes (re-visioning). Their chapter is a narrative history that traces how seminal ideas and practices emerged.

This is followed in Chapter 2 by Nicky Marshall's account of how the archetypal figure of Chiron – the wounded healer – is alive and well at Re-Vision. It is one of those old stories which tell a healing tale for those falling apart and who are willing to unravel. Her tale tells of how wounds are the mothers and fathers of destiny.

In Chapter 3, Ewa Robertson's Third Body is a sensitive alignment of neuroscience with soulmaking. She revisions the notion of the 'Third' to give it a somatic yet transpersonal base. She defines this Third as, 'the body that therapist and client share whilst being independent of it and one another'. The moving case study she uses exemplifies this subtle working with body.

From here we move into Chapter 4's 'The Garden of Love', in which Sarah Van Gogh explores the soulful uncertainty involved in therapists being prepared to not-know and how through immersion in the relationship, a deep kind of love shows itself. In this richly fictionalized case study, she and her client together find a William Blake poem at the centre of their work.

In Chapter 5, Chris Robertson takes us into the deep end of soul making, its need for a poetic speech, for deep pathos and the intimacy of the heart. He explores how soul wants to experience all the details of joy and suffering; delights in beauty and accepts its ugliness; wants to dwell in the vale of soul-making, as Keats called it. This vale is where the personal and collective intersect.

Joan Crawford outlines in Chapter 6 the vital importance of ecopsychology for a reawakening and participatory engagement with the pain of the world in contrast to the dissociated view of 'if we are fucked, better make the most of it'. She highlights dreams of *borderland* (as opposed to *borderline*) clients that carry messages to us from the ecological unconscious and how therapists can struggle to validate these.

In Chapter 7, Jo-Ann Roden brings a process style of writing that mirrors the non-linear, apparently chaotic work of psychotherapy with soul. She follows Hillman's line with revisioning pathology and, as she does, she illuminates the dark corners of the soul and reveals something of the creative struggles and dreams of her own journey.

Mary Smail's magical venture through the mythical language of stories in Chapter 8 shows how the simplicity of story offers a numinous companionship for both client and therapist. She gives a glimpse of how story can facilitate an unconscious process beyond that of the therapist's ego control.

In the final chapter, Chris Robertson attempts a look underneath what is already an 'underworld' work. He posits an *inter-experience* as essential to a different kind of knowing in relational psychotherapy that fits the idea of the 'Third' explored throughout this book.

Chris Robertson & Sarah Van Gogh
September 2018

---

[1] James Hillman, *We've Had a Hundred Years of Psychotherapy – And the World's Getting Worse* (New York: HarperCollins, 1992).

[2] Rainer Maria Rilke, 'You, Darkness', in *Book of Hours: Love Poems to God* (New York: Riverhead Books US, 1997).

Chapter 1

Roots and Seeds

Ewa Robertson and Chris Robertson

Re-Vision was born on 12 June 1988 out of a series of consecutive dreams that we had over a two-week period during 1986. The dreams were about a second part to our wedding that we hadn't planned for. We had no idea how to prepare for it. What garments were we to wear to the initiation ceremony? We might say that we were *being dreamt*. One night one of us would have the dream, the other continued the dream the following night, and so it went on. Something *other* came through us that we could not have anticipated; it didn't feel like it was *our* doing. We were in the grip of a shared dream that held a *telos* – a sense of being touched by fate. While the mystery of the dreams had to be incubated they carried an implicit intentionality that we were compelled to give birth to, yet had no idea how to prepare for or what to expect. Far from having any extrinsic goals, we were following a path that was unfolding as we walked it.

Re-Vision's name came with the inspiration of needing to really look again, to see things with new eyes which, after all, are the windows to soul. Our opening ceremony was on 11 September 1988. The dream was still unfolding as we were bringing it into form. Initially we ran short courses for personal and professional development. There were no thoughts of offering a whole counselling and psychotherapy training. However after a couple of years, we were encouraged by qualified therapists who attended our courses to run a full training programme and 'grow our own'. The daemon or spirit that was dreaming us was relentless. It took time to 'get it' and be courageous enough to take it on.

We had years of experience behind us from previous trainings – humanistic, psychodynamic, family systems and psychosynthesis – but the dream demanded a letting go of established ideas and

concepts into a formative creative period. If we were about to em-
bark on a training anew, what sort of training would we like to have
been in ourselves? This became a guiding question. *Re-visioning*,
the willingness to look again, was seminal to the unruly spirit of
Re-Vision. Without explicit rules and expectations as to what con-
stitutes a counselling or psychotherapy training (professional ac-
creditation was in its infancy), we had to reach for innovative
inspiration. The process was itself probably the key method –
opening the doors to what was waiting at the threshold: the guest
invited or uninvited, needing hospitality. It was wildly creative and
brought many difficulties and mistakes along with it. A *trust in the
emerging process* and a *willingness to learn though experience* would
become two of the hallmarks of the Re-Vision craft.

We each had different areas of interest and experience – Chris
was drawn to archetypal psychology, Ewa to the developmental.
There was a tension between these two – the archetypal emphasizing the essential as in the emergence of what was in the 'seed'
and the developmental pointing to thresholds that are potentially
transformative. Within a therapeutic context, an archetypal perspective allows seeing through to the necessity of the shape of a
person's life – not an aim as in some ego goal, but discovering the
underlying meaning of why it needs to be just as it is. This perspective cuts through neurotic notions of victimhood or dominance. As James Hillman describes in his 'acorn' theory, we have
an inherent calling that subtly weaves life experiences towards the
imperatives of soul.[1]

The developmental perspective not only provides a framework
for understanding how we grow a sense of self in the context of
our environment and negotiate critical thresholds, but also enables us to gain an understanding of the unique psychological process of individuation from the perspective of soul. Both the
developmental and archetypal aspects, while different, offer lenses
for seeing the soul's journey.

As part of the integrative framework, we saw their difference
as a creative tension and wove these opposing yet complementary
poles together to form a foundation of what underpins the ethos
of our training. Holding the creative tension became a template

for learning to work with many types of difference. This became intrinsic to the training, and Re-Vision has held conferences on various themes relating to working with difference and diversity. As a training team we held disparate views, which meant we could avoid collapsing into a monoculture.

In January 1991, on the day of the start of the Persian Gulf War, we launched the counselling and psychotherapy training programmes with our first cohort of 18 students. Since then there have been hundreds of counselling and psychotherapy graduates. Like any birth, Re-Vision has been a labour of love needing support along the way, which we write about later on.

Coming to counselling for the first time as a client, or starting a psychotherapy training, requires a leap into the unknown. Many graduates of Re-Vision acknowledge that if they had known what radical demands the training would make on them beforehand, they might not have had the courage to start. In our safety driven culture, starting something you cannot prepare for in advance may look like folly. Setting off on an unknown journey is like that of the Fool of the Tarot starting his/her journey into the unknown with a trust in whatever will emerge. We too found ourselves, like the Fool, having faith in the journey as we set off. We were on a steep learning curve that included many inevitable errors. Hillman writes how *ananke*, necessity, brings errors into our paths to shape destiny.

> If this errant cause, necessity, is the principle in errors, then let us consider error necessary, a way the soul enters the world, a way the soul gains truths that could not be encountered by reason alone. Psychological awareness rises from errors, coincidences, indefiniteness, from the chaos deeper than intelligent control.[2]

Along with what seemed like chaos came synchronicities deeper than any intelligent control we might have exercised. Our learning curve was not simply acknowledging errors but understanding the deeper psycho-spiritual context within which they were a necessary part of our maturation. Re-Vision itself became a crucible for this deep learning in which the soulful perspective could be a lived experience.

Drawing on Systemic approaches developed in Family Therapy, and in particular the work of Watzlawick on change, we deepened our capacity to accept errors.[3] We drew attention to the probability that 'mistakes' that a client (or even the therapist) make are potentially significant if understood within a different context – for instance, empathic failures by the therapist may act as catalysts to 'second order change' that disrupt the relational system (see Ewa Robertson's case example in Chapter 3 of this volume). Context is a seminal notion that includes frame and the potential for reframing, but also holds meaning laden with the potentials for soul making – as Hillman says in the previous quote, 'let us consider error necessary, a way the soul enters the world'.

Each therapy session is an interplay between conscious and unconscious dynamics between therapist and client and within each of them. This is paralleled with the connection/alignment, or lack of it, between ego and soul. Part of the therapist's task is to sense the emergent possibility within that connection. A common way of explaining this is seeing the opportunity in every crisis. Unfortunately such a simplistic formula can lead to a sort of positivistic terrorism in which the client has their painful experience disallowed (see Figure 1.1).

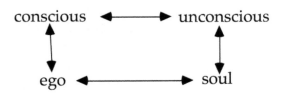

Figure 1.1. The dynamic relationship within the therapist.

While relying on there being an adequate therapeutic alliance in which containment, contact and rapport are present, the skills of contextualizing build the possibility of a connection between the client presenting an issue in therapy and the implicit experience of meaning. Just as empathy entails adapting to the client's lived world, so this connection entails seeing through their persona to a deeper story. 'Seeing through' means not being assimilated into the rehearsed narrative that the client is telling, but imagining how this 'problem' might function within the soul's poetic movement. Although perhaps implicit in systemic reframing, context now functions as a catalyst for soul making. An example of seeing through is given later in the work with 'Susan'.

Since its beginnings, Re-Vision has 'seen through' the upward thrust for growth and expansion of consciousness that typified the Human Potential Movement and Transpersonal Psychology in the 1970's and 80's as part of a heroic notion of development that we believe also plays out in unsustainable industrial growth. We see 'growth' as driven by the masculine ego that wants to expand, dominate and control and, by default, denigrate the feminine. John Welwood coined the term 'spiritual bypass' as a description of spiritual development that seeks to avoid painful psychological wounds.[4] Our focus was on growing *down* rather than growing up, on *deepening* rather than transcending, coming *into* our bodies rather than going beyond them. In keeping with this, as an organization, we wanted to remain small and grounded to avoid the risk of running away with our excitement. We found ourselves drawn to feminine principles such as vulnerability, embodiment, immanence, containment, shadow and, of course, soul.

We understood the feminine (soul) to be denigrated and marginalized in a culture that had become driven through an inflated masculine intoxicated with spiritual energies. We drew on the work of Jungians and post-Jungians with such titles as: *The Return of the Goddess*,[5] *World As Lover, World As Self*,[6] *Descent To The Goddess: A Way Of Initiation For Women*,[7] *An Image Darkly Forming: Women And Initiation*,[8] *The Heroine's Journey: Woman's Quest For Wholeness*,[9] *Addiction To Perfection: The Still Unravished Bride*,[10] *Re-visioning Psychology*[11] and *Care of the Soul*.[12] These texts honour the sacred in beautiful and moving ways that fitted the emerging frame of a new training.

Anthropologist Victor Turner, whose explorations of initiation rites are seminal for understanding liminal states, became another central tenet of the developing theoretical framework.[13] Bani

Shorter's work on border transits was inspirational in helping conceptualize the crises that specifically characterize such crossings.[14] But, undoubtedly, much of the thrust of Re-Vision's difference came from the work of James Hillman in his challenge to the idea of 'growth' in therapy, in his warning of the dangers of spirit without soul, of the normative hazards of developmental theory, of the medicalization of pathology, and his challenge to a belief in any formal training in psychotherapy![15] Taking on such challenges helped hone the craft of being willing to look again and re-vision many accepted ideas.

While drawing on this rich vein of Jungian writing, our emphasis was on craft rather than concepts. We explored how to translate the beauty of these ideas into the practice of working therapeutically. Here we drew on the humanistic traditions, especially gestalt, in facilitating groups to learn through experiential process and thereby own the ideas authentically. We named this process *inside-out learning*. In this learning style the development of therapy skills is first presented in an implicit experiential way and only later made explicit. Building on inner knowing is part of the *inside-out* learning method in which students learn to trust their intrinsic experience rather than using it as a means to an end. Re-Vision does not expect students to reinvent the wheel and rediscover everything that has already been mapped in counselling and psychotherapy, but they are encouraged to make learning their own through rooting it in their subjective experience. Students are invited to see the models and conceptualizations we offer as transitional objects, which support them on their way to their own insight.

One of the challenges for training organizations is that of students who feel exposed for some failure or difference that did not fit with the teaching. Conformity to a norm that reflects the modality can easily appear in groups, resulting in the creativity of difference going underground – into the shadow. This is where the 'inferior' gets pushed out and soul is denigrated in favour of egoic progress and success. To imagine that the most vulnerable, least successful part of us is somehow central to our being is not easy. What if that which is currently seen as the most difficult, most awkward, most despised part of a person (as many myths and fairy stories testify), is actually a vital part that has something precious to offer? This idea that what has been marginalized into the shadow has the potential for transforming the whole is an essential Re-Vision seed.

Students are imbibers of the organizational culture, both consciously and unconsciously. So where the agendas of the training are instrumental (success, large group numbers, status for trainers), this attitude will be reflected in graduates' work in the wider community. Elsewhere, Chris Robertson has documented the dangers of dysfunctional attributes in training centres.[16] Becoming aware of the differential power issues, not just within individual psychotherapy but also within the training, is vital for a healthy organization to be able to function creatively. Failure to address these matters can result in students complying with the accepted 'norm' and repeating this pattern in their clinical work.

Learning to listen to and hear the marginal, shadow voices became an important principle and also an essential part of the craft. This parallel between delivering training and the psychotherapeutic practice we were teaching, became a critical tool of reflective practice. We wanted to walk our talk, to practice what we were teaching, and the difficulties in doing so became part of the learning craft. By making a space at Re-Vision to recognize the shadow side of transpersonal energies (heroic tendencies to inflation, dominance, being invulnerable), we attempted to both serve the flame of our vision and seek help in recognizing and working with the inevitable shadow. In terms of the organization this entailed building in 'backstop' structures, including having an outside supervisor, who could catch and reflect back blind spots. In terms of therapeutic practice this meant developing sensitivity to the marginal voices within the client as well as the discounted, unheard voices within the community.

While it is normal practice in supervision to reflect and deconstruct the therapist's agenda, shadow issues become amplified when they are held within the lens of the training as a whole. The consistent wider lens helps hone the practice of listening to the margins. It is like the eye adjusting to darkness; when the pupil opens, the eye can take in what is in the twilight of the in-between zone. The seminal theme of exploring the margins and hearing whispered messages of shadow material has continued to be integral to our approach to psychotherapy.

One of Re-Vision's first courses was entitled, 'The Borderlands and the Wisdom of Uncertainty', which in 1990 became the subject of a BBC documentary. This course explored the junction points where normal laws fail to operate – a liminal space where old means of self-regulation do not work but new ones have not yet been developed. These 'borderlands' lie, like their territorial counterparts, in an in-between reality that is not governed either by what has come before or what is yet to be. While being chaotic in nature, they are a source of creative potency. Crossing into a therapist's consulting room can be a crossing into that liminal space, where the usual social conventions do not work. Winnicott considered such transitional spaces to be the location of cultural transformation.[17] Psychotherapy has long explored events that constellate at boundaries or transitional spaces, starting with the sacred dreams that took place in Greek temples. The mysterious, chaotic nature of these thresholds has a dream quality and requires us to move into an imaginative mode, attending with peripheral vision to unexpected flashes from another reality.

A significant innovation in this course was the use of ritual to create a sacred and holding space for those passages through liminal transitions. The rituals are not formalized and do not belong to any particular religion or spiritual heritage. They are participatory and inclusive. Together the group constellates a sacred space by simple mindful actions such as walking a circle or making an offering. One example is a grief ritual in which participants formulate statements of attachments to out-dated dysfunctional habits and symbolically let go of what they have collected by placing them into a grief box, which is then released.

Every culture has its rituals. In traditional societies these take the form of initiation rites to mark a threshold.[18] Some formal, secular rituals in our western culture seem empty in comparison – for example, sitting in an examination hall for hours and silently writing answers to questions. Not surprisingly many young people self-initiate by inventing their own rituals, though these can be extreme and dangerous. As therapists, we frequently hear stories of ritualized self harm and abuse accompanied by feelings of shame and humiliation.

For many years now, Re-Vision has held an annual conference. In 2008 the conference title was *Sacred Margins*. The programme read:

> The theme of this conference is *liminality*, the borders between worlds, described by anthropologist Turner as *betwixt and between* and by Winnicott as *transitional space*. Psychotherapeutic approaches that explore such border territories require the therapist to be able to dwell in this twilight zone where their rational mind has no passport. These sacred margins are the subject of this conference.
>
> We intend to explore such questions as:
>
> • How does psychotherapy interface between the inner and outer worlds?
>
> • Can the language of *transference* adequately describe the subtle phenomena encountered at the borders of consciousness?
>
> • Does (statutory) regulation weaken psychotherapy's capacity to tune into the undercurrents of the collective?

This emphasis on what is at the borders – between the conscious and unconscious, between therapist and client, between the therapeutic couple (of therapist and client) and the wider culture – has developed from those early seeds in the 'Borderlands and Wisdom of Uncertainty' course into a major ingredient of the training. In our increasingly disordered and fragmented world, the capacity to manage anxiety and tolerate uncertainty has become increasingly relevant. The emphasis on a release from conscious knowing, on relinquishing the place of the expert, opens up the vitality of learning together. It is not a question of equality, as clearly there is a power differential both between client and therapist, and between students and trainers. It is an appreciation of the *mutuality* of a creative interaction whose outcome holds inevitable uncertainty. It became apparent that to hold such uncertainty, there needed to be containment. At the organizational level, this grew with the sense of working with a professional community who were committed to the ongoing work of re-visioning.

As a young organization we were lucky enough to attract a circle of respected elders who supported and worked with us to provide the holding containment for the vision. This group included: Barbara Somers, founder of the Centre for Transpersonal Psychology; Ursula Fausset, founder of the London Gestalt Centre: Irene Bloomfield, founder of The Raphael Centre; and Miceal O'Regan, founder of Eckhart House Dublin – all sadly gone yet we remember and are grateful for their wise counsel. They reminded us, time and time again, to walk our talk and step out of the way, to listen to the voice of the exiled, to stay open to feedback even if it wasn't comfortable, and to dare to speak our truth. We met fortnightly with Barbara Somers, who helped us think through the shape and structure of the training, facilitating our stylistic differences and reminding us to 'save our breath to cool our own parsnips' whenever we became over-heated and reactive.

We have always placed a high value on community, welcoming feedback and being true to our name by remaining as open as we can to learning. At the organizational level we were blessed to work with a professional community who were committed to the principle ethos of re-visioning so that within a few years it was no longer just the two of us. Letting go of ownership continued in various ways and at various stages. In 1997 we handed over our roles as directors and Re-Vision became a charity. As well as having outside professionals, graduates were eligible and encouraged to become trustees to include their skills and experience in the overall ownership. Re-Vision has grown into a self-regulating community of relationally orientated people who bear witness to the heart and soul qualities that symbolize the organization.

Community as a container allows for connection as well as differences. Respect for differences are so often the grit in the oyster, the discomfort that leads to change. Martin Buber referred to the 'Essential We' as a community built on each member taking personal responsibility where authentic meeting takes place.[19] He writes 'the sicknesses of the soul are sicknesses of relationship'.

Relationships are a powerful modulating variable. Donald Winnicott stressed that healthy communal life means taking care and responsibility for the well-being of others in the group.[20] In an ego dominated world, this means moving beyond ourselves and relating meaningfully to one another. We then become morally accountable to the wider world.

Drawing on psychodynamic practice as part of Re-Vision's integrative perspective was part of what supported this deeper sense of the holding required to work with fragmented states, such as clients with borderline characteristics, or those in midlife crises. The similarity and key differences between what Wilber called 'pre-ego' and 'trans-ego' states became an early identifier of Re-Vision practitioners, whose craft enabled them to work with a wide spectrum of disturbance.[21] This critical distinction between those with pre-ego needs and those needing to release old defences, found an immediate place within Re-Vision's wheel model, the cycle of initiation that we developed through Turner's three phases of initiation – *crisis, liminality* and *return*. Figure 1.2 is an example of the Re-Vision wheel model that came to be seminal in our approach. The image of a wheel emphasizes the cyclical nature of development. We do not develop in a straight line but by going through difficult and painful issues again and again. This may look like a compulsion to endlessly repeat (and sometimes feels that way) but the wheel is an image of returning to issues at ever deeper levels.

There are three thresholds on the wheel that represent turning points when one phase transits to another. On the first threshold, *Separation*, a shift depends on there having been sufficient grieving of idealized hopes to allow the longing for autonomy to call us onward. Similarly, at the second threshold, *Liminality*, there needs to be a willingness to surrender control to the longing for the Beloved (for whom the heart yearns). And lastly at the *Return*, there is a necessary grieving for the potential loss of that heightened state of union, in order to feel the pull of human companionship with all its challenges.

The first and second thresholds mark similar but qualitatively different changes, characterized by psychological birth and death. In the first threshold, the individual separates out from infancy

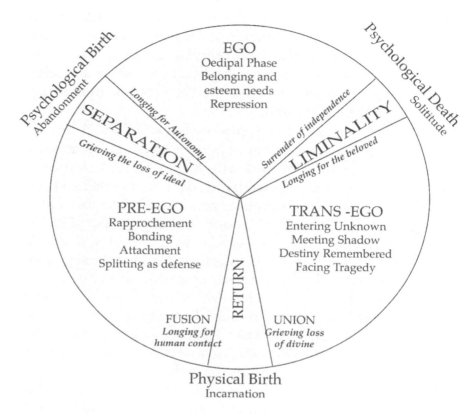

Figure 1.2. The Re-Vision Wheel, the cycle of initiation.

and childhood and emerges from the matrix of family life through a process of individuation, to meet the challenges of their unique path in life. In contrast, psychological death marks the surrender, at least for that round of the wheel, of control and ego-driven goals, to allow a dissolving into a larger sense of identity and belonging – to being part of the whole.

A practical example of working at thresholds with a composite client named 'Susan' was given in Freshwater & Robertson.[22] Susan was in a crisis of identity and anxious about who she really was behind her social masks. The therapist considers different ways of understanding her anxiety, which lies between the fear of annihilation that stems from not having been mirrored as an infant and the existential challenge of being seen as her true self. Either way, the anxiety is the same but the meaning is different, because the context is different. Initially the therapist hears her anxiety of being abandoned by him as belonging to the pre-ego dimension, of replaying her father's emotional and physical abandonment. Thinking in terms of the pre-ego phase, he wonders aloud if she is afraid of expressing her desire to be close because it seemed to replay her situation with her father. In this intervention he displaces the uncomfortable possibility that it might be her feelings for him as a person.

The dream that she brings to her next session awakens him to her existential dilemma. She is attempting to escape from prison but the chains on her ankles slow her down. At a critical juncture, the guard at the exit does not stop her but offers her back the golden coin she had surrendered on entering prison. Her waking ego does not consider the golden coin significant in comparison to the escape. The therapist wonders if she is attempting to escape the responsibility for the gift she was not ready for when she entered. Will she now take responsibility for it? This is a shift of context towards the existential dilemma of self-betrayal that takes the client and therapist into the trans-ego threshold.

While no model can mirror the complexity of a therapeutic encounter, the wheel illuminates the distinction between the pre-ego fear of non-being and the trans-ego anxiety that accompanies release from the prison of internalized expectations. It also highlights the difference between a neurotic shame connected with sexuality, and the shame of not being true to oneself (self betrayal). The complexity lies in the fact of these two not being as distinct in practice as they are in theory.

Although at the time when this was originally written, it was intended solely as an example of individual therapy, 'Susan' could be seen as a personification of Re-Vision facing into its existential challenges. Just as individuals are required to face the challenges of their soul journey, particularly those involving betrayal, so has Re-Vision, and through that process has matured and grown down. Over the 30 years of its development, Re-Vision has pioneered the development of a soulful approach to the *craft* of counselling and psychotherapy that attempts to bridge the psychodynamic with the sacred, the developmental with the archetypal. Offering an integrative pluralistic model of the psyche, the key ideas that have endured and been explored and elaborated further in these chapters are: *inside-out learning, liminal space, shadow, the synergetic 'field' and the Wounded Healer*. In more recent years this has extended to include the relational heart of psychotherapy in terms of embodied psyche, including more recent advances in neuroscience (see Chapter 3, 'The Third Body', by Ewa Robertson), ecopsychology (see Chapter 6, 'Rediscovering our Kinship with Nature', by Joan Crawford), and the archetype of the Wounded Researcher (see Chapter 2, 'The Wounded Healer', by Nicky Marshall).

We hope that this opening chapter has outlined something of the history, or better *myth-story*, that has taken shape and is being constellated at Re-Vision. To refer back to our first prospectus (1988), the course description for the course entitled 'Psychosynthesis of the Heart' read:

> The path of the heart is the welcoming back of that from which we have separated ourselves. Through pride, fear and ignorance, we have abandoned the Cinderella within us into darkness. In doing so, we may suffer the reactions of our violence, hatred, envy, isolation and despair. In this course, we will address these symptoms as collective and personal phenomena that cry out for redemption and healing. Through acceptance and forgiveness, we can learn to reopen the channel of love to the dark side of our nature.

After many years of nurturing the training at Re-Vision as founders, we started a process of relinquishing power and control to others. As previously mentioned, an important first phase was setting up the charity in 1997. The second was in stepping back from the executive that managed the training under the auspices of trustees. The last one, current to the writing of this book, is our complete retirement from training commitments at Re-Vision, having ensured a good handover to others who form a talented training team. Despite many turbulent and difficult passages along the way, it is wonderful that Re-Vision has established a viable niche within the counselling and psychotherapy field that honours soul. This has not been easy within a culture where extrinsic goals, the quick fix and commodification are rampant. From its visionary start, Re-Vision has grown down into this marketplace with a vibrant call for psychotherapy to reclaim working with soul. While its integrative programme has drawn from many current psychotherapy modalities, Re-Vision has forged its own identity.

The gift that was carried in that sequence of original dreams has flowered and new seeds are growing.

The Seed Cracked Open

It used to be
That when I would awake in the morning
I could with confidence say,
"What am 'I' going to
Do?"

That was before the seed
Cracked open.

Now Hafiz is certain:

There are two of us housed
In this body,

Doing the shopping together in the market and
Tickling each other
While fixing the evening's food.

Now when I awake
All the internal instruments play the same music:
"God, what love-mischief can 'We' do
For the world
Today?"

—Hafiz[23]

[1] James Hillman, *The Soul's Code: In Search Of Character And Calling* (New York: Random House, 1996).

[2] James Hillman, *Re-Visioning Psychology* (Oxford: Harper Perennial, 1977), p. 160.

[3] Paul Watzlawick, *Change: Principles of Problem Formation and Problem Resolution* (New York: Norton, 1974).

[4] John Welwood, *Towards a Psychology of Awakening: Buddhism, Psychotherapy and the Path of Personal and Spiritual Transformation* (Boston, MA: Shambhala, 2002).

[5] Edward Whitmont, *Return of the Goddess* (New York: Crossroads, 1982).

[6] Joanna Macy, *World as Lover, World as Self: Courage for Global Justice and Ecological Renewal* (Berkeley, CA: Parallax, 1991).

[7] Sylvia Brinton Perera, *Descent to the Goddess: A Way Of Initiation For Women* (Toronto: Inner City Books, 1981).

[8] Bani Shorter, *An Image Darkly Forming: Women And Initiation* (London and New York: Routledge, 1987).

[9] Maureen Murdock, *The Heroine's Journey: Woman's Quest For Wholeness* (Boston, MA: Shambhala, 1990).

[10] Marion Woodman, *Addiction to Perfection: The Still Unravished Bride* (Toronto: Inner City Books, 1982).

[11] James Hillman, *Re-Visioning Psychology* (Oxford: Harper & Row, 1975).

[12] Thomas Moore, *Care of the Soul; A Guide for Cultivating Depth and Sacredness in Everyday Life* (New York: Harper Collins, 1992).

[13] Victor Turner, 'Betwixt-and-Between: The Liminal Period in Rites de Passage', in *The Forest of Symbols: Aspects of Ndembu Ritual* (Ithaca, NY: Cornell University Press, 1967).

[14] Bani Shorter, *An Image Darkly Forming*.

[15] James Hillman, *Re-Visioning Psychology* (1975).

[16] Chris Robertson, 'Dysfunction in Training Organisations', *Self & Society* 21, Issue 4 (1993).

[17] Donald Winnicott, *Playing and Reality* (New York: Tavistock Publications, Routledge, 1971), pp. 95 – 103.

[18] Richard Frankel, *The Adolescent Psyche* (London and New York: Routledge, 1998).

[19] Martin Buber, *Between Man and Man* (New York: Macmillan, 1965) p. 202.

[20] Donald Winnicott, *Maturational Processes and the Facilitating Environment* (1963; Abingdon and New York: Karnac, 1990).

[21] Ken Wilber, *Up From Eden: A Transpersonal View of Human Evolution* (Abingdon: Routledge & Kegan Paul, 1981).

[22] Dawn Freshwater & Chris Robertson, *Emotions and Needs* (Buckingham and Philadelphia, PA: Open University Press, 2002), pp. 88 – 89.

[23] Hafiz, 'The Seed Cracked Open', in *The Gift: Poems by Hafiz*, translated by Daniel Ladinsky (New York and London: Penguin Compass, 1999).

Chapter 2

The Wounded Healer: Chiron as Mythic Guide to the Practice of Therapy

Nicky Marshall

Why bother with myth? Myths matter. Myths tell stories of archetypal figures and of universal themes about what it means to be human, animal, divine. They are blueprints and maps of the psyche and offer us access to an imaginal realm that bypasses our rational ego-mind and allows us to revision what it means to be who we are; to make meaning out of experience and see a purpose in the 'slings and arrows of outrageous fortune' we are pierced by.

> Myth preserves a common human memory... These myths of good and evil bring together the varied intuitions arising from human life. They unite the intellectual intuition people have about the world around them with the experiential knowledge they gain about themselves... As stimulants to personal involvement they awaken a uniquely individual way of knowing... Myth shows the challenge awaiting each person.[1]

Myths are an essential source of deepening insight into life. Jean Houston defines myths as '... something that never was, but is always happening... Myth waters our every conscious act and is the very sea of our unconscious life'.[2] The myths we attend to and invoke have an influence that our conscious minds cannot direct or anticipate.

If, with James Hillman, we share the view that the craft of therapy is an archetypal practice, we are then hopefully drawn to ponder the nature of the archetypes that we invoke when we sit in the room with our clients. If we '... imagine archetypes as the deepest patterns of psychic functioning, the roots of the soul governing the perspectives that we have of ourselves and the world...', it becomes important to know the mythic and archetypal influences that hold sway, and which imbue each therapeutic field with a particular quality when therapist and client sit together and explore the nature of the suffering that brings the client to therapy in the first place.[3]

Whilst there may be many archetypes that are at times constellated in the practice of therapy – confessor, teacher, midwife, mother, father and muse are just a few that spring to mind – Re-Vision, since its inception, has given a primary place to that of the Wounded Healer, to the myth of Chiron and the guidance that the story offers us. I hope through this chapter to give the reader some insight into the themes of the myth, their relevance for the practice of therapy, and the value of holding to its images and metaphors in the crafting of a therapy that attends to soul, one which respects wounds and symptoms as the gateway to, and the voice of, soul. In this context I am again invoking Hillman and using the term 'soul' as he does, to refer to 'that unknown component which makes meaning possible, turns events into experiences, is communicated in love'.[4] To explore the myth and its relevance for therapy in a way that is congruent with the Re-Vision approach, requires us to start with a personal encounter with the myth, with an evoked experience rather than a body of theory. So, to place soul at the heart of the work, we will begin with the language of soul – image, story and metaphor – and attend to the myth itself.

The Myth of Chiron

Chiron was the child of Philyra and Cronos. Philyra was desired by Cronos, and to escape his unwanted attention she changed into a mare, but Cronos changed himself into a stallion and mated with her, returning afterwards to his wife on Mount Olympus. When Chiron was born, immortal as a God, but in the form of a half human, half horse Centaur, Philyra was distraught and pleaded with the Gods to transform her into other than she was – this they did, turning her into a Linden Tree.

The sun god, Apollo, adopted the orphaned Chiron, who grew

to be the noblest and wisest of the Centaurs. He became adept in the arts of healing, leadership and music. Many heroes and gods gave their sons into his care so that he could educate them in these noble arts. On one occasion, he healed Telephus of a wound that had been caused by a spear that Chiron himself had made, fulfilling the prediction of Apollo's Oracle, that 'the wound could only be healed by its cause'.

One day, Hercules visited the centaurs and persuaded one, Pholos, to open the most precious wine; the other centaurs were angry that it had been drunk, and in the fight that ensued, Hercules fired an arrow that struck Chiron in the knee, in the animal part of his body. The arrow had been dipped in the poison of the hydra, and so caused a fatal wound. But because Chiron was immortal, he could not die, and the wound couldn't heal. Howling with the pain, Chiron withdrew to his cave, and attempted all the remedies he knew to heal the wound, but nothing worked. In his unceasing quest to heal, Chiron travelled far and wide, learning many new things and healing the ills and wounds of many others, but with no release from his own suffering.

Eventually Hercules pleaded with the gods to release his friend from the suffering that he had caused him. The gods relented, and a deal was struck. The gods allowed Chiron to take the place of the Titan Prometheus, who had been chained to a rock as punishment for stealing fire from the gods and giving it to humans. Every night an eagle would peck out his liver, and every day it would regrow. Hercules fired an arrow, killing the eagle and releasing Prometheus. Chiron descended into Hades, where he remained in the underworld for nine days and nights. At the end of this time, Zeus took him from Hades and set him in the heavens as the constellation of stars called Sagittarius, where he remains to this day.[5]

'Our only health is the disease'[6]

So, what meaning does this story have for the practice of therapy? Much therapy is Apollonic – rational and thoughtful, for 'Apollo is the god of rational enlightenment, objectification and intellectual distancing'.[7] If we practice counselling and therapy

29

with Apollo as our guiding deity, we will know much and be skilful, but our practice may lack a depth of soulfulness, may seek to find an answer and to resolve the conundrums that present themselves, but be less able to be with uncertainty and not knowing, to develop negative capability, that capacity described by Keats 'of being in uncertainties, mysteries, doubts, without any irritable reaching after fact and reason'.[8] The myth of Chiron, with its many images, is a more soulful guide for Re-Vision therapists. In our training and in our practice, he has much to offer, and with which to challenge us. We need to attend to the images and themes embedded in the story, to understand, and to stand under them, to allow them to resonate, and to come into relationship with them.

Chiron is initially 'wounded' through the story of his conception and birth, abandoned by father and mother, a being from the worlds of the gods, humans and animals, and yet belonging nowhere – a creature of the borderlands and liminality. We might reflect on what it means that he is fathered by Cronos, the god of linear time and thus of his-tory (or her-story), suggesting perhaps that it is the stories that we tell ourselves about our origins that can leave us with unhealed and untended wounds.

The figure of Philyra is the only personified image of the feminine in the story, so it would be wise for us to pay attention to her. Despite her attempts to outwit Cronos, he succeeds in his ravishing of her, and in her distress at the appearance of her son, she is changed into a Linden Tree. We might allow this part of the story to remind us that we are all wounded in our early relationships, that some element of abandonment and mis-attunement is an inevitable companion to life, an existential wound. This perspective, which recognizes that we are all wounded, is vital in the Re-Vision model. It reminds us that we walk common ground with our clients. It helps us to remember that 'I'm not OK, you're not OK (and that's OK)!'

Perhaps this part of the myth enables us to recall, with Hillman, that we might re-frame our thinking, seeing ourselves not only as 'wounded by our parents' but also as 'parented by our wounds'.[9] Within this context we might see some of the work of therapy as being to support the client (and ourselves) to tell a different story, so that our 'history' becomes a more Healing Fiction – for all the stories that we tell in therapy are more or less fictional, after all (which is not to say that they are lies).[10]

This awareness of our own wounding is crucial if we are to avoid the trap that Guggenbuhl-Craig describes.[11] He writes of the dangers of healing being located in the therapist and woundedness only being located in the client. He cautions us to remember that clients have the capacity to constellate healing within themselves, and that for us to identify only with the healing aspect of the archetype robs the client of this healing factor in themselves. It is important to recall that no one ever 'heals' another: a physician does not heal a broken bone – he or she can only create the optimum conditions for the healing potential within the bone itself to have the best chance of succeeding. This recognition of our mutual experience of woundedness creates a place for meeting in relationship.

Staying with Philyra, and staying close to the image, we might ask what meaning it has that she is turned into a Linden tree, and no other, for images are always specific: in varying cultures the Linden tree is considered sacred, and also believed to be a tree of truth – anything spoken under the shade of the Linden tree could not be a lie.[12] This could serve to remind us again of the sacred nature of our wounding, and that our wounds speak a certain difficult truth, and so are to be honoured in the work, not simply seen as a problem to be fixed.

> There is a pain – so utter –
> It swallows substance up –
> Then covers the Abyss with trance –
> So Memory can step
> Around – across – upon it –
> As one within a Swoon –
> Goes safely – where an open eye –
> Would drop Him – Bone by Bone[13]

Adopted by the sun god, Apollo, Chiron is 'fathered' by intellect, rationality and reason; the noble arts and wisdom become his domain. Through these defences against the pain, he 'rises above' the early wounds, achieving much and becoming widely recognized for his skills and gifts. Within the Re-Vision frame this speaks to the phase of the Wheel of Initiation in which we move out from our earliest 'story', developing an identity and an ego (along with the shadow of that conscious identity) to create a place for ourselves in the world, but often at the cost of having to deny, compensate for, and repress our initial wounds, as the poem by Emily Dickenson (above) so graphically articulates. It's during this part of his journey that Chiron makes the sword that wounds Telephus, the wound which only Chiron can heal. This is an illustration of the idea that we can only be healed through an encounter with that which has wounded us – if our early wounds are created in the cauldron of relationship, this part of the story suggests that it is only in the context of a relationship that healing can take place. As Yalom says, '... it's the relationship that heals'.[14] This is a central element in the Re-Vision approach to therapy, which attends closely to the quality of the relationship.

For many of us, during this mid-life phase of our journey, the achievements and rewards of ego gradually begin to wear thin, but there will come a moment, often in mid-life, when we are seemingly doing well, when life, the Gods, Soul, comes knocking, and our carefully constructed life and defences fail us and the repressed returns.

'Things fall apart, the centre cannot hold'[15]

In the myth, this is the shocking moment when Chiron is wounded in the knee by the arrow fired by Hercules, his friend, and one of the noble young men he had mentored. Attending closely to the imagery of this part of the story, we are reminded that life can indeed deal us shocking and unexpected blows, that life may be changed in an instant, with the sudden death or terminal diagnosis of a loved one, the loss of a job, our health, the future we had in some way expected to have. Chiron is wounded by Hercules, his friend. Perhaps this asks us to see those who wound us not as enemies but as friends – that wounding may be a service and thought of as the gift of a friend, not necessarily the disservice that ego would label the experience. Chiron is wounded in the knee, the 'horse part' of him. This speaks to a compensatory function of the mid-life wounding, drawing attention as it does to the 'inferior' part of Chiron, that which links him to his origins and to his animal nature, which has been ignored in favour of rationality, learning and 'the noble arts'.

Our present culture, with its addiction to growth, expansion and the pursuit of 'happiness', tends at this point to look for as fast a return to the status quo as possible. A therapy based on the importance of a strong and functional ego identity as an end in itself, rather than a necessary phase in our journey through this 'vale of Soulmaking', will bid for normal service to be resumed as soon as possible. Such an approach tries to hurry us through our encounters with loss and grief in all its forms, and limits our periods of mourning. The result is a grief that is retroflected, turned inward in depression, and leaving us longing only for a time past, unable to respond to the pull towards a deeper and more nuanced encounter with ourselves, for 'When grief remains unexpressed... it hardens, becomes as solid as stone. We in turn become rigid and stop moving in rhythm with the soul'.[16]

If we permit this aspect of the myth to be our guide, we resist the (understandable) call to frame suffering as 'the problem' which needs to be fixed, and instead strive to hold a perspective that honours symptom as the voice of soul calling to be heard. We trust that the wound is the gateway to the soul. This asks us to stay humble, not to identify with the role of 'healer', thus leaving the client only holding woundedness. In this we need to allow the pain of our limitation, to bear disappointment, inadequacy, not knowing – to trust in the value of negative capability.

> *I sit with Peter – he has been referred by his employer for support. His first child was stillborn. He describes carrying the tiny coffin into the chapel for the funeral service. He cries, heart-rending sobs. All he wants to know is 'why?' My eyes fill with tears, and I don't hide them. I feel my own impotence to make the slightest jot of difference to his grief. I*

stay present, allowing the pain in my own heart. I say, 'Not knowing why... and knowing that question can never be answered... is unbearable'. As an empathic statement, it, and by extension, I, feel totally inadequate, but I stay silent, allowing this infection, the connection with my own experiences of being unable to do all that I would have wished to for my children. In this space, as I bear witness to his grief, something tender begins to shift in the energy of the room. He breathes, and makes eye contact, his body softening a little.

Peter's cry of 'why' and his outpouring of grief was his manifestation of the part of the story where we see the images of Chiron withdrawing to his cave, 'howling in pain'. A grief such as his is a painful illustration of the long struggle to heal that which cannot be healed. My own feelings of impotence in sitting with Peter, and my resonance with his grief were excruciating – the almost visceral pull to action of some sort was intense – although what action is there to take in this moment? Michael Kearney writes something of this in 'Becoming (and Sustaining) the Bodhisattvas We Already Are'.[17]

He writes of sitting with a dying man, for whom all attempts at pain relief are failing, and how '... for many years, I have been helped in my clinical practice by the image of 'the wounded healer', one who chooses to stay... with his or her own pain and sense of impotence', that staying with our own pain, and being fully present to the suffering of the other, can awaken the potential for healing.

> The wounded surgeon plies the steel,
> that questions the distempered part[18]

Whilst fruitless from the perspective of an ego seeking a quiet life, Chiron's attempts at self-healing ultimately gift him with greatly enhanced skills in easing the suffering of others. From our Integrative Transpersonal perspective, the images and motifs from this part of the myth tell us much about the necessary attitude towards both our own wounds and those of others. It reminds us of the need to attend to that which ails us, not in order to 'fix' or eradicate, but to come into a different relationship.

In his search for self- healing, we may imagine Chiron repeatedly attending to the open wound in his knee, salving and binding it, coming slowly and painstakingly into a different relationship with that which hurts and bleeds. This motif asks us to come into a different relationship with our griefs and hurts, to tend, clean and salve them. Within our understanding of the way in which healing comes about, this process repeated over time, builds the psychological equivalent of healthy scar tissue. As practitioners it allows us to trust that we can be present to our own pain in a meaningful way, allowing our scars to be a humbling reminder of our own vulnerability. This creates a mutuality in the therapeutic process and an ability to trust in the process of therapy, in the therapeutic relationship, and the potential for healing that is constellated by attention to what is wounded.

The building of scar tissue allows us to trust that we can enter into the pain of woundedness, and re-emerge, that we will not be lost forever in the suffering. So often clients fear that if they begin to connect to their pain, grief, rage and despair, they will fall forever into the abyss. Knowing the metaphoric process of 'scar formation' offers us a different perspective. We can make the shift from 'nursing' our grievances, that is holding on to them, where we make the mistake of 'falling for our stories' to a 'tending' of the wound that gives it a place.[19] This facilitates the redemptive move from defence against consciousness of the wound to an appropriate capacity to protect when needed.

Also of relevance here is recognition of the reciprocity of wounding and healing – without a wound, there would be no healing. If wounds are the gateway to soul and to a deeper encounter with our interior world, we need to give them a place and trust in their importance. We need our wounds to know our soul. By coming to know the soul-making capacity that is engendered through our descent into the depth of our wounds, and the redemptive potential in the return, we can come to trust in our recognition that '... the study of lives, and the care of souls means above all a prolonged encounter with what destroys and is destroyed, with what is broken and hurts'.[20] By extension this also asks us to trust that at times we may have to have the courage to wield the 'Subtle Knife' that cuts between the worlds of denial and 'the place where it hurts', so that in recognizing the wound we can open a way for healing to begin.[21]

Mary tells me yet another story of how she has, once more, spent time that she has had to create through endless self-sacrifice, in doing things to make life easy for her teenage daughter. They have a painfully fragile relationship, for which Mary feels responsible, having made choices in the past that left her daughter feeling unloved and unwanted. Now Mary does everything possible to prove her love and care. I hear each week how she exhausts and distorts herself to do this. I have my own story of a wounded mother-daughter relationship. I know the place that would do anything to have had things be different. My heart aches in resonance with Mary... and yet... I take a deep breath:

'You love and care for your daughter so much... and you would do anything for her, to make her happy... and no matter what you do, and how hard you try... nothing can make it be so that the past didn't happen. You can make the present and the future different, but you can't change the past.'

She stills, and stays silent. The session ends. I feel her vibrating with rage as she leaves without her usual goodbye. I wonder what will happen. Will my words, my naming of what is true, end the relationship? (Which is, of course, the fear that prevents Mary from speaking anything that might challenge her daughter. She is held hostage to her love, and the fear of losing it).

The next week she arrives as usual and sits in her chair. She looks me in the eye. 'I can't begin to tell you how much I hated you last week. When I left I wasn't going to come back. But I have thought about what you said all this week, and it's true... I can't undo what I did.' For the first time in therapy her eyes fill with tears, and she begins to grieve for what was lost, for that which was not chosen in the choices that she made. The potential for healing is constellated as the grief is given a place, no longer denied through the unconscious belief that actions now can undo those of the past.

It is important to ask 'what is it that transforms a wounded person into a wounded healer?' Or perhaps more accurately, into a vessel, through which the archetype of the Wounded Healer can manifest.

Firstly we need to be able to recognize our own woundedness, and to be able to sustain sufficient contact with our own pain that we are not defending against it, but neither are we overwhelmed by it – this is the value of 'scar tissue'. When first struck by the arrow, Chiron is overwhelmed by the pain and seeks to retreat from it, but over time he is able to bear it enough to travel the world in search of a cure. As we strengthen our ability to stay present to our own suffering we are less prone to project our wounds onto others. It is this ability to bear with ourselves and not need our clients to be the only wounded ones that supports our efforts to stay authentic, and not hide behind a professional persona. This creates greater potential for authentic meeting, and the constellation of a relationship that heals. A therapist who is avoiding their own pain will unconsciously teach the client to do the same, yet it is the client's wound that bought them to therapy and which needs attention.

Secondly, we need to be receptive to the pain of the client, and allow our own wounds to resonate with that. The image of Chiron's open wound illustrates a place of sensitivity and of access to the inner world. It is thus an imaginal representation of empathy,

> ... it signifies an archetypal image of an empathic consciousness which is in its own way, a wound; a wound that brings consciousness. The therapist's very capacity for empathy his ability to 'feel into' and share the patient's inner life also lays him open to become wounded.[22]

A therapist who is afraid of their client's pain will unconsciously teach the client that they are too ill, too bad, too pain-filled for the therapist – or indeed anybody – to handle. We need to trust the healing process, a trust that develops through our own experiences of descent and return. This requires a certain courage, not of a heroic nature, but in the deeper meaning of the word, connected to heart, which brings compassion for the task. We need to be willing to allow our woundedness to be of service, to be a vessel for the containment and acceptance of the client's suffering, so that it becomes possible to reflect and thus make meaning from the story of their wound, to tell it consciously, rather than act it out unconsciously. Through this, the potential for transformation can have a place. Healing comes not by 'treatment' but by not being afraid of wounding, and through being willing to enter the wound *beside* the client. Again, quoting Kearney,

> ... the healer that I already am is fluid, interconnected and ever changing – that healing is not something that I personally do to or for another. Healing is what naturally happens when we (the other and I) become part of the fluid, interconnected, impermanent, always-changing process that is ultimate reality. [23]

We might sum this up more succinctly by recalling that often the most important thing to do in the work of therapy, and the hardest thing to learn, is to keep out of the way of the process!

Thirdly, we need to be able to bear with the uncertainty of what is happening in the work, to trust that we are mutually held by something bigger than ourselves, that while we may hold our client, we are held in turn in a bigger story, a mythic dimension. An image of this holding from popular culture occurs in the film *Superman*, when Lois Lane falls from a building and he scoops her up – he tells her it's OK, 'I've got you', to which she not surprisingly replies, 'Yes, but who's got YOU?' The moments of grace when we know that we are part of a larger story, that we are participants in and held by a mystery where we don't have to know all the answers, are the sacred spaces in which healing occurs.

Fourthly, a stance that holds to the ethos that symptom is the voice of soul and sees the symptom as a way to attend to the unfolding soul story of a lifetime, asks us to deconstruct some of our modern medicalized attitudes to suffering. This requires us to render 'psychopathology' back to its etymological origins, its deconstruction into 'the meaning of soul's suffering', and to redeem diagnosis from being something that one (expert, 'healthy') person does to the suffering of another (sick) person. It needs instead to be thought of in its original sense of 'deep knowing', a knowing that our wounds and distress offer to us if we are willing to stay with the pain.

To work in this way we need to find the capacity, as Joanna Macy says,

> ... not to run from the discomfort and not run from the grief or the feelings of outrage or even fear and that, if we can be fearless, to be with our pain, it turns. It doesn't stay static. It only doesn't change if we refuse to look at it, but when we look at it, when we take it in our hands, when we can just be with it and keep breathing, then it turns. It turns to reveal its other face, and the other face of our pain... is our love... our absolutely inseparable connectedness with all life.[24]

Our willingness to try and stay present to pain, even if we are not always successful, to reflect upon our 'failures' and to try again, begins to support a shift from a causal frame to one of responsibility, the beginnings of the move from the victim place of 'why me?' and of blaming the other, to the transformational frame of responsibility and choice. This moves us from the hell of meaningless suffering to the possibility of seeing that there is a meaning and a purpose in what happens. Ego may never get beyond a desire to have it be different, but from the perspective of soul, there is a gift in our woundedness, and a meaning to soul's suffering.

> I said to my soul be still
> And wait without hope
> For hope would be hope for the wrong thing.[25]

Finally, after all of the work and the struggle, there comes a moment of surrender, expressed in the myth by the hero Hercules' request of the gods to release his friend from his perpetual torment and to allow him to die. We might read this as a necessary humbling of the ego, which opens the way for Chiron's descent into Hades, the underworld where he rests and waits for nine days and nights. We might follow Hillman here, seeing this descent into the underworld as essential, for '... the dimension of our soul-travel is downward'.[26]

The releasing of Prometheus suggests too that there is a necessary end to some suffering. We might think of the eagle as a metaphor for the neurotic suffering which we can endlessly cause ourselves – the pain that comes from trying to avoid the pain. It is this that needs to recognized, so that we can move from the heroic, repetitive neurotic level of our wounds to the surrender, descent and 'in-dwelling' of the time in the underworld.

Within the Re-Vision Wheel, the Cycle of Initiation would be represented by the threshold between the Ego phase of development and the Trans-ego phase. On this edge we come to a place of acceptance, a recognition that what has served us in the past now limits and constrains us. We begin to see that our struggle against this surrender is causing us more pain that the surrender itself may do, to see, with Anais Nin, that '... the risk to remain tight in a bud was more painful than the risk it took to blossom'.[27].

This threshold – the turn into the pain, the descent into Hades – is, from the perspective of ego, a movement that we don't want to make, for, as is suggested by the time spent in Hades, it is a death of what was before. All internal change is the death of ego identity as we know it, and ego always fears its own death. But from the viewpoint of soul, such a turn into depth is precisely what is needed.

During the Re-Vision five-day residential retreat in which this myth is explored in depth by students at the end of their second year of training, this liminal transition is marked by an overnight ritual, in which they are invited to hold and reflect upon the question: 'What is the gift of my wound?'

The following morning they share the responses to the question that have arisen, in the form of a poem, a ritual return that is always deeply moving. I have permission from the author to include one such poem here, which articulates the capacity to bear with our own wounds, if we engage in this process over time, and with consciousness:

I do not fear the fall

Last night I dreamt of a bird
With broken wings
Whose fall from flight was inevitable
Who fought to fly
But fell at last
And landed
In a coat pocket
A soft, padded landing.

I have fallen so many times
My own wings broken by life's heavy load
And each time I have fallen I have met the ground
The ground that has caught me when no one else has
That gave me the permission to rest in the sweet relief
of letting go
That held me
Through my wailing sorrow and despair
That never turned its back on me
The ground that softened me
Opened me
Before strengthening me
And readying me
To return and rise again
I do not fear the fall.[28]

At the end of this time of waiting without hope in the dark, Zeus takes Chiron from the depths of the underworld, setting him in the heavens in the form of the constellation of stars we call Sagittarius. The myth is silent on why Zeus acted in this way, on 'what happened' to effect the transformation, but in this we can see an affirmation that the willingness eventually to surrender the struggle, and trust in the unknown, opens us to those moments of mystery and grace that are amongst the hallmarks of a Transpersonal therapy.

Many years ago I worked as a therapist in a community drug and alcohol project. One day I received a referral from a local residential rehabilitation service. Helen, a single woman in her early 30's, had successfully completed a six-month programme and was returning to live at home. She wanted support to manage the challenges she would face in staying sober.

Helen's story included a difficult childhood, growing up with erratic parents, and a mother with mental health problems. She had two younger siblings that she regularly protected from her mother's unpredictable outburst. At 13 she discovered that alcohol helped numb the pain. By the time she completed university she was developing a significant dependence on alcohol and a variety of illegal drugs. Despite this she functioned well in the world and became a team leader in a social service Child Protection team.

We could see here the parallels with the mythic themes of Chiron, the early wounding and the attempts to salve and rise above the pain of the wounds, through substance use and the compensatory role of a competent and crusading protector of vulnerable children.

She began a relationship with a man who also had substance misuse and mental health problems, and the relationship rapidly became violent and dangerous to her, physically and emotionally. She began having substance induced blackouts and several times ended up in sexually risky situations. At this point she recognized that she was dangerously out of control of her substance use. She began to face up to the first step of recovery in the 12 step approach – that she was powerless in the face of her addiction – in other words ego could no longer find ways to manage, to keep the chaos at bay, to defend against the wounds of childhood – it all came crashing in.

Helen was lucky in the rehab that she was able to go to – it was the only one in the area whose clients were exclusively women and was run alongside an order of nuns. Sadly it has since closed for lack of resources. The centre operated on a basis of demonstrating care and respect for the residents, many of whom had lost all capacity to care for and respect themselves – essentially the staff loved the residents, despite all their efforts to be unlovable. Every woman entering the rehab was appointed a prayer sister, a member of the convent who would pray specifically for her appointed partner during her time in the rehab and beyond.

In entering the rehab, stepping out of the world and turning in to face the pain of her story, Helen, like Chiron, surrendered to a descent, and stepped over the threshold between the world of ego and the trans-ego realm of spirit and soul. Every woman who completed the rehab programme was sent back into the world through a ritual transition in which she was presented with a butterfly pin, as a symbol of transformation – akin to the image of Chiron being transformed into the constellation of Sagittarius.

When we began meeting it was as though Helen, having left rehab had returned to the world anew, was engaged in a recycling through the birth/death threshold of the wheel of initiation. The work for us was to come into relationship and build an alliance, and as that progressed she began to explore again her early stories, and also the shame of the abusive relationship she had been in. After several months she met someone through the AA fellowship and began to open to the possibility of relationship with him. One Monday morning she called and asked for an emergency appointment. We met that afternoon and she talked about having been away with her new partner. The relationship had become sexual, her first clean and sober sexual relationship. Perhaps that was why, during the night she had suddenly had a flashback to being sexually abused by a friend of her parents, when she had been around 11 or 12. Shocked and distressed, she nonetheless began to make connections between the repressed experience of the abuse, and some of the subsequent events of her life – the drinking at such a young age, the repeating patterns in her adult relationships which might be understood as the neurotic attempts to avoid and unconsciously master the original traumas. She also began to reflect upon the call to work to protect abused children – an unconscious redemptive calling, an attempt to create a purpose to her own suffering.

Although these memories opened the connection to another, deeper layer of early trauma, her experiences of finding the courage to face into and to sit with the pain of her feelings in the rehab allowed her to trust that this new pain from her returning memories would not overwhelm her, that it too could be faced and that something transformative would emerge from the journey back into the depths. She trusted her ability to form a healthy scar.

Over the next few months we worked to explore her rage at what had happened, to see the impact of the past and the legacies of the abuse, and to support her in staying able to care for herself, to stay clean and sober, and to process and de-toxify the shame that she felt, coming eventually into a loving and caring relationship with the young part of herself that she had previously shut away. We came to see that this was both the part that had been projected onto the children she had worked so hard to save and protect, and the seed that flowered into a passionate desire to be of service to others.

About six months later she decided to move to live with her partner in another part of the country and our work had to come to an end. In our final session we reflected upon her journey of recovery, the parts of herself that she had come to know, and her growing capacity to hold them with compassion. We stood together again on the death/rebirth threshold, both of us feeling the sadness of the ending of our relationship, and the hope for the future. She began to speak about what it meant for her to have recovered the missing part of her story, and to reclaim the child part of her that had been split off from consciousness in the abuse. Shortly before the session ended, she said, 'You know, what happened to me wasn't right, and I don't forgive him... but... what happened is part of what made me who I am... and for the first time in my life, I like who I am. So, I can't wish that it hadn't happened, because that would mean wishing to be different, and I won't go back there again. I guess that's all there is to say about it, really.'

Helen's story is a recapitulation of the Chiron myth and a journey into depth that I was privileged to share part of. The myth is one that we all live out in one way or another as we journey through the world. If we are lucky, our wounds draw our attention inwards and into our own depths, into a lived connection with soul, where we might find the love that is the other side of pain, the wholeness that emerges from our shattering, and the joy that is the other side of grief. It is the place where we learn the truth of the poem:

The Unbroken

There is a brokenness
Out of which comes the unbroken.
There is a shatteredness out of which blooms
The unshatterable.
There is a sorrow beyond all grief
Which leads to joy
And a fragility out of whose depths
Emerges strength.
There is a hollow space too vast for words
Through which we pass with each loss
Out of whose darkness we are sanctioned into being.
There is a cry deeper than sound
Whose serrated edges cut the heart as we break open
To the place inside
Which is unbreakable and whole,
While learning to sing[29]

[1] S. D. Breslauer, *Martin Buber on Myth – An introduction* (London and New York: Routledge, Taylor & Francis Group, 2015), p. 154.

[2] Jean Houston, *Myths for the Future*. Audio Cassette (Sounds True Incorporated, 1995 edition).

[3] James Hillman, *Re-Visioning Psychology* (New York: HarperPerennial, 1992), p. xix.

[4] Hillman, *Re-Visioning Psychology*, p. xvi.

[5] Traditional version of the Myth of Chiron, retold by the author.

[6] T. S. Eliot, 'East Coker', from *Four Quartets* (London: Faber and Faber Ltd., 1944).

[7] M. Whan, 'Chiron's Wound: Some Reflections on the Wounded-Healer', in Nathan Schwartz-Salant and Murray Stein, eds, *Archetypal Processes in Psychotherapy* (Wilmette, IL: Chiron Publications, 1987), pp. 197 – 208.

[8] John Keats, 'Letter to his Brothers', 1817, quoted in 'Negative Capability', *Keats' Kingdom*, at http://www.keatsian.co.uk/negative-capability.php (accessed 19 July 2018).

[9] James Hillman, 'Puer Wounds and Ulysses' Scar', in *Puer Papers* (Irving, TX: Spring Publications Ltd., 1979).

[10] James Hillman, *Healing Fiction* (Dallas, TX: Spring Publications Ltd., 1994).

[11] Adolf Guggenbuhl-Craig, *Power in the Helping Professions* (Thompson, CT: Spring Publications, 1983).

[12] 'Lime tree in culture', *Wikipedia*, at https://en.wikipedia.org/wiki/Lime_tree_in_culture (accessed 19 July 2018).

[13] Emily Dickinson, *A Choice of Emily Dickinson's Verse*, ed. Ted Hughes (London: Faber and Faber Ltd., 1968).

[14] Irving Yalom, *Love's Executioner and Other Tales of Psychotherapy* (New York: Basic Books, 2012), p. 112.

[15] William Butler Yeats, 'The Second Coming', in *Selected Poetry*, ed. A. Norman Jeffares (London: Macmillan, 1962).

[16] Francis Weller, *The Wild Edge of Sorrow: Rituals of Renewal and the Sacred Work of Grief* (Berkeley, CA: North Atlantic Books, 2015), p. 19.

[17] Michael Kearney and Radhule Weininger, 'Becoming (and Sustaining) the Bodhisattvas We Already Are', in Koshin Paley Ellison and Matt Weingast, eds, *Awake at the Bedside: Contemplative Teaching on Palliative and End of Life Care*, pp. 125 – 135 (Somerville, MA: Wisdom Publishing, 2016).

[18] T. S. Eliot, 'East Coker'.

[19] Hillman, 'Puer Wounds and Ulysses' Scar'.

[20] Hillman, *Re-Visioning Psychology*, p. 56.

[21] Philip Pullman, *His Dark Materials* (London: Yearling, 2001), Book 2.

[22] M. Whan, 'Chiron's Wound', p. 202; pp. 197 – 208.

[23] Kearney and Weininger, 'Becoming (and Sustaining) the Bodhisattvas We Already Are'.

[24] Kearney and Weininger, 'Becoming (and Sustaining) the Bodhisattvas We Already Are'.

[25] T. S. Eliot, 'East Coker'.

[26] Whan, 'Chiron's Wound', p. 202; pp. 197 – 208.

[27] Anais Nin, https://www.passiton.com/inspirational-quotes/6743 (accessed 19 July 2018).

[28] Meredith Husen. Stage 2 student 2016.

[29] Rashani Réa, 'The Unbroken', *A Year of Being Here*, 26 October 2014, at http://www.ayearofbeinghere.com/2014/10/rashani-rea-unbroken.html (accessed 19 July 2018).

Chapter 3

The Third Body

Ewa Robertson

A Third Body
A man and a woman sit near each other, and they do
   not long
at this moment to be older, or younger, nor born
in any other nation, or time, or place.
They are content to be where they are, talking or
   not-talking.
Their breaths together feed someone whom we do
   not know.
The man sees the way his fingers move;
he sees her hands close around a book she hands
   to him.
They obey a third body that they share in common.
They have made a promise to love that body.
Age may come, parting may come, death will come.
A man and a woman sit near each other;
as they breathe they feed someone we do not know,
someone we know of, whom we have never seen.
Robert Bly[1]

True to its name, the training at Re-Vision has been *re-visioned* and
lived through many incarnations throughout its 30 year history,
yet some core ideas such as soul, the synergetic field, Eros and the
wounded healer have remained fundamental to its evolution and
form the bedrock of its theoretical framework.

My own contribution to the central structure of the training
has been a weaving of these principles together with others drawn
from my interest in contemporary and relational psychotherapy,

A version of this paper was first presented at the Brighton Therapy Partnership
in February 2018.

developmental and attachment theory, and neuroscience. What links all of these in my teaching and clinical practice is embodiment. To quote Merleau-Ponty, 'It is through my body that I understand other people'.[2] In this chapter I explore these ideas with a case example and what I will be conceptualizing as the Third Body.

My original training was in Psychosynthesis. Its founder Roberto Assagioli viewed the body, emotions and thoughts as 'instruments' of experience, perception and action which, if disidentified from, freed one to no longer be 'enslaved to the body' but instead be 'a Centre of Will, capable of mastering, directing and using all my psychological processes and my physical body'.[3] After more than 35 years as a practising psychotherapist, supervisor and trainer I have come to the opposite view. I have come to recognize and value the place of body, mind and emotion as the ground for a lived experience of soul. In the ancient Greek myth, Psyche and Eros gave birth to Voluptas, the goddess of 'sensual pleasure'. I offer her here as an image of an embodied psyche or an ensouled body.

From its start, Re-Vision has followed a more Jungian trajectory into the depths of the human psyche, acknowledging the many ideas fashioned by Jungians and post-Jungians. While giving a place to the development of the ego and its defences as well as the place of spirit, our focus is with soul.

Soul

Soul and psyche share the same etymological roots in Greek. James Hillman writes 'Soul, psyche, anima and animus (unlike 'self', which is a more abstract and reflective symbol) have etymological associations with body experiences and are concrete, sensuous and emotional, like life itself'.[4] To avoid the notion of soul as a 'thing' or an entity, it is better to speak of *soulfulness*, *soul-making* or *ensouling*. In other words, a quality, a movement, a process. Hillman calls soul 'a perspective rather than a substance, a viewpoint toward things rather than a thing itself'.[5] Soul is about depth – we are in touch with soul when we are moved to our deepest thoughts, feelings and embodied experience. Soul connects us to our deep humanity.

In the myth of Psyche and Eros, Psyche's labours involved a profound encounter with darkness and despair. Many traditional myths follow a similar path of psychic transformation with a downward journey. Dante Alighieri, in his *Divine Comedy*, lost in a forest in darkness, follows Virgil on a path of descent. The Sumerian goddess Inanna and the Greek goddess Persephone also undertook journeys of descent into the underworld. Often in life we are faced with challenges we hadn't anticipated with no outer map to guide us. Psyche, Dante, Inanna and Persephone were unequipped, symbolically naked and unprepared for their journeys, yet connected with a source deep within to guide them.

Soul is experienced at the meeting point between inner and outer, or as Novalis writes, '... soul is where the inner world and outer world touch'.[6] This in-between space is an area that holds many creative possibilities which I go on to explore.

Field

Another central idea and practice at Re-Vision is that of the field, also known as the intersubjective, interactive or synergetic field. The idea of the field, originally a term used in physics, refers to the energetic flow of unconscious psychodynamic forces.[7] This way of thinking is concerned with the nature of human interaction occurring in an in-between space, Winnicott's intermediate area.[8] The field is the shared reality, the shared subjectivities of therapist and client, two subjects each with agency. Analytical psychology extends this view to also include the intersection of the subjective with the collective unconscious, making the interactive dynamic horizontal in the interpersonal realm and vertical in the transpersonal. Murray Stein writes: 'The field becomes a *presence* that both people are inside of and, simultaneously, observers of'.[9] From this perspective, the terms transference and countertransference, although relevant, become limited since the therapist is entangled with what happens within the field and simultaneously is aware of it.

As therapists, we attune and pick up cues empathically to inform us of what is going on in the client's inner world and its regulatory influence on the relationship. We recognize mood and affect, and that sensitivity often shows up first as a response in our own body. Allan Schore writes '... the clinician's body is a primary instrument for psychobiological attunement and the reception of the transmission of nonconscious affect'.[10] Our bodies are reading cues all the time, including what has been split off or dissociated. We pick it up in imagery, sensations (such as hunger, sexual arousal, nausea), feelings (such as anger, grief, boredom, love, frustration), or fleeting fantasies. Much of this rapid nonverbal communication takes place outside of our awareness yet is being communicated backwards and forwards nonverbally between therapist and client. For example, we can detect the subtlest of changes in facial expression within a 100 milliseconds and instantly mirror this back.[11] Depending on the context, we refer to this unconscious communication as projection, projective identification, transference and countertransference – all of which provide useful sources of information. From an embodied perspective, field dynamics is an intersubjective engagement of two bodies and two psyches.

Importantly it is the therapeutic relationship itself that is pivotal and transformative. Lewis Aron,[12] Stephen Mitchell,[13] Stolorow and Atwood,[14] Jessica Benjamin[15] and other contemporary psychotherapists emphasize the intersubjective engagement as that which enables deep structural changes to occur. The true power of healing is not conceptual or outer but comes from within.

Since the therapeutic relationship is a mutual bi-directional process it necessarily means that the therapist must be willing to participate in the process of change, growth and healing.

The Wounded Healer

Working with field dynamics means being receptive and open to the unconscious communication that is occurring in the therapist-client relationship. The relationship becomes the crucible for change and contains the therapeutic couple.[16] Crucibles are subjected to very high temperatures. The therapist's use of self to enter into another's reality is likely to mean being subjected emotionally and somatically to the transfer of all kinds of intense, difficult, disturbing, or painful states and feelings. Re-Vision's inside-out learning approach (see Chapter 1, 'Roots and Seeds', by Robertson and Robertson) means a willingness to be open to one's own wounds as part of the healing process. Healer, heal thyself. As with Chiron the wounded Centaur, unless we recognize our own suffering and can bear this pain we will not be able to truly empathize or be with another's suffering. Without a connection to our own woundedness the best we can attempt is a symptomatic cure which is not the same as healing. The extent to which the therapist is in touch with and can allow their own vulnerability and be a wounded healer, will influence the extent to which the therapeutic relationship itself can be a healing one.

Following Stephen Mitchell's proposal, by becoming part of the problem we become part of the solution and healing process.[17] This means a willingness to *become part of the change process*, in other words, to *be* changed by the process. Jung refers to the inevitability of the therapist being psychically infected:

> For two personalities to meet is like mixing two different chemical substances: if there is any combination at all, both are transformed. In any effective psychological treatment the doctor is bound to influence the patient; but this influence can only take place if the patient has a reciprocal influence on the doctor. You can exert no influence if you are not susceptible to influence.[18]

And further on, Jung notes, '...the doctor is as much 'in the analysis' as the patient'.[19]

Wilfred Bion,[20] Donald Winnicott,[21] Thomas Ogden[22] and others have highlighted the importance of the therapist remaining open to a creative potential space, to be able to enter a 'reverie'; that is, to be open to seemingly random thoughts and responses as clues to what is being co-created in the therapeutic field. More recently Jessica Benjamin has stressed the importance of the therapist's surrender to the mutual reciprocal influence of the therapeutic couple with its inevitable enactments and impasses.[23] This way of working and thinking about the therapeutic couple involves more than simply referring to our own state in order to gain information about the client's inner world. That can still be a subtle way of maintaining distance. It means a letting go of seeing oneself as the expert, or in Lacan's words, 'the one who knows'.[24] Jung, in a similar vein, said of the therapist: 'No longer is he the superior wise man, judge, and counsellor; he is a fellow participant who finds himself involved in the dialectical process just as deeply as the so-called patient'.[25]

With findings from neuroscience we are increasingly recognizing the extent to which we are connected to one another. Adrienne Harris echoes the view of many contemporary theorists that 'people in dialogue actually are profoundly enmeshed'.[26] Just as neurons in the brain and nervous system connect across synapses, so we might think of humans (ant and bee colonies are good examples) connecting across social synapses.[27] For better or worse, we regulate and shape one another. We interactively regulate positive or negative states of being, positive or negative states of emotion, across these social synapses. In terms of brain systems, the premotor cortex and mirror neurons – the parts for detecting others' feelings and for registering our own – are largely overlapping. These days I use the term transpersonal to include the transmission of emotional and affective states between people or even with other-than-human beings. I suspect we are more permeable and interconnected than we yet know.

Eros

Eros, the god of relationship and relatedness, has caused much controversy in the world of psychotherapy – abused, sexualized, shamed, sanitized, repressed, transmuted. However we think of Eros, Eros is a feature of all relationships and in the consulting room brings a quality of immediacy and aliveness. Eros is intimately connected with our vitality. Thomas Moore writes about our desire nature, sexual fantasies and longings as being messengers of the soul.[28] Psyche and Eros belong together, initially united unconsciously in darkness but later, when Psyche brings an oil lamp to set eyes on Eros, they are bound together in a conscious encounter. Through suffering, the wound Psyche inflicts on Eros leads the way to his becoming human. In turn, Psyche is touched and transformed by the divine. As Neumann puts it, 'The tale of Psyche ends with the deification of the human Psyche... and so likewise Eros... through suffering prepares the way for union with the human Psyche'.[29]

In psychotherapy, in each human encounter, we engage Eros as much as Psyche. Understanding Eros from the perspective of soul, we come to see longing as a yearning for love, for what the Sufis refer to as the Beloved, our essential wholeness.

Third Body and the Space Between

The commitment to an embodied intersubjective dialogue implies surrendering to a bigger process. Out of the two a third body emerges, referred to also as the analytic third, the third area, or simply the Third and which I refer to as the Third Body. The notion of the Third has been used differently by different theorists.[30] I am using the notion of the Third Body along the lines that Jane Burka suggests as 'the body that represents the *shared unconscious life* of the therapist/patient *pair*'.[31] This Third Body is an emergent property of the relationship, often born out of an unexpected change in rhythm or feeling tone. It is born out of the space between the therapist and client, 'generated by (between) the separate subjectivities of analyst and analysand', yet is neither owned nor created by either one.[32]

Dean

I've anonymized as much as possible Dean's story in order to protect client confidentiality. Some of it is a composite of clients, though the images, and specifically the animal images, are true to what happened and for which I have the client's permission.

Dean was a street fighter and frequently in trouble with the law. He came to therapy because he didn't want to 'go back inside'. He was avoidant and aggressive in the extreme with a menacing stare. He always wore black, and always a T-shirt with a wild animal print. I offered him a very early morning appointment.

The therapist's body is a valuable resource and bank of information about the client's intrapsychic processes. Dean had implicitly learned that aggression was his best coping strategy. His entire presentation, verbal and nonverbal, spoke of his history without my knowing many significant biographical details at the beginning of our work together. Whilst I found his energetic presence intimidating it told me of the need for control, underlying fear and sense of danger he lived with. This was the relational field we inhabited.

Dean had a dim view of psychotherapy and often made condescending remarks about my efforts to reach him. It was as if I was with a predatory animal and I could easily become his next prey.

> *'Tell me about your childhood?,' I said, attempting to encourage him to tell me more about himself. 'How old were you when you first started fighting?'*
> *'None of your business, babe. What's past is past. No point crying over spilled milk, is there? Got to get on with life.'*

I realized that if Dean and I were to connect meaningfully something had to shift so that the dance we were in of dominate or be dominated had a chance of *real change*.

By focusing exclusively on the verbal narrative and ignoring or avoiding the body, the client's or our own, we split off part of ourselves. This limits what is possible in the relationship and gets communicated subliminally back to the client.

Somehow I had to get *into* the crucible with Dean. What I hadn't anticipated was how my body would become part of the dance. Working relationally we are often working at the edge of our comfort zone.

> *At the end of our fourth session I got up to accompany Dean to the door. As the door closed behind him I became aware of something hanging from the back of my trousers. Toilet tissue. That morning had been a terrible rush. I was mortified at the loss of control of my body; I felt exposed.*

Had he seen the toilet tissue? He must have registered it at some level. This was just the sort of ammunition Dean was capable of using to humiliate another, and pour scorn over all that 'psychobabble rubbish'. I felt I had failed him and myself. Was I ever going to be able to regain a sense of my integrity, my dignity?

I dreaded the next session but I knew I had to let go and be open to what came. This was a moment of my surrender, acknowledging and not avoiding my own vulnerability. As the doorbell rang I reminded myself of the therapist's adage 'trust the process and breathe...'

The first thing I noticed was that Dean was wearing something different, still an animal print on the front of his T-shirt but it was a cartoon character, a Tasmanian Devil called Taz. I later discovered Taz has a friendly side to him but I didn't know that then. Was it my imagination or was there a softer look around his eyes? Without thinking, I smiled. He responded with an awkward smile. There was a pregnant pause as if we were on a cusp.

Dean and I were reading one another's facial and other non-verbal cues and this subtly influenced how close or distant, open or defended we were in any given moment. Roz Carroll describes Beebe and Lachmann's understanding of interactive regulation to involve

> ... a finely-tuned subliminal level of *coordination between two people*, involving split second responsivity of face, gaze and head orientation. This complex and continuous communication, paralleled in mother–infant and thera-pist–client relationships, has come to be recognised as a result of micro-analyses of interactions between human beings in many contexts. The rapid, non-conscious, im-plicit and coordinated exchanges between pairs reveal how much relating is based on anticipation of the other, adjusting, and responding... Beebe and Lachmann's con-cept of interactive regulation is a term which describes the process of coordination between self and other

THE THIRD BODY

across a range of possibilities from the extreme of non-coordination (disconnection) to very high coordination (vigilant or merged).[33]

Quite unexpectedly Dean spoke of an alcoholic and violent uncle who raised him. This uncle had unpredictable rages. Once when Dean was a young boy he took a broken bottle to his face, then smashed everything in his bedroom including all his toys.

> 'I can't imagine how that made you feel.'
> 'It was crap,' was all he could say but that was enough to help me start to feel into what the young Dean had experienced at the hands of his sadistic uncle.
> 'Crap?' I asked, wondering if I might need that toilet tissue after all.
> 'He'd just explode out of nowhere; however hard I tried to stop it it happened every time; I couldn't help myself. He'd go ballistic.'
> 'Sounds really terrifying.'
> I noticed his shoulders curl inwards and matching him, mine did too. He seemed to lose control of his body posture and slumped backwards into the chair. We both exhaled.
> 'Yeah, I couldn't help it. It would all get out of hand. It always did. He said he'd shove my face in it. He didn't mince words.'

What was it he couldn't help? I didn't need to ask and he never said but I filled in the gap for myself with the violent images of what terror can do to your body. Putting his 'crappy' feelings together with the toilet tissue, the contempt I often experienced from the uncle introject, the shame his and mine, the feeling of threat and terror, I felt at last the dots of his verbal and nonverbal narrative were joining up.

I found Susan Sands' statement helpful: 'the patient and I succeeded in co-creating in me a state in which I could 'get' something viscerally about the pathogenic interactions of his childhood that he unconsciously needed me to understand'.[34]

Dean needed me to *get* in *my* body/through *my* body what he couldn't put into words. We had co-created in me what he needed me to know and understand. Without intending to I became part of a powerful enactment as it played out through my body. An intellectual understanding of projective processes was insufficient to help me process what was happening at an emotional and bodily level. It required surrender on my part, a willingness to be in touch with my vulnerability and trust in a bigger process.

> *Whether or not Dean had been aware of the toilet tissue something had irrevocably changed. We had moved from a polarized you/me position to a sense of* we. *Now I noticed for the first time his handsome well proportioned facial features, the scar above his eyebrow, the unusual yellow green colour of his eyes. We were allies at last: he looked at me; I looked at him. For the first time I felt really open to him. I was still looking into the eyes of a wild animal but we could hold each other's gaze. He was no longer about to attack.*
>
> *My tummy gurgled in response to the release of tension and I knew he heard it too. I didn't tighten my body this time. It spoke for both of us. He reached into his pocket and pulled out a bag of muffins and handed them to me.*
>
> *'Did you have time for breakfast this morning?' he asked.*
>
> *I paused. 'It's good to feel cared for, isn't it?' I said to both of us.*

So how did that shift happen? To quote Benjamin, 'the analyst's surrender means a deep acceptance of the necessity of becoming involved in enactments and impasses'.[35] As difficult and shaming as it was to find the toilet tissue, I managed to remain open sufficiently to what was to happen next. In the field what belonged to whom was less distinct. Through the enactment Dean no longer had to bear the shame alone; he no longer had to experience the dread of the loss of control of his body or project this fear on to others. In the moments of the most intense affect as he described the violence he was subjected to at the hands of his uncle, I connected to fleeting images and associations of degradation and terror of my own. Dean had made the descent past his familiar defence mechanisms to a deeper level of his unconscious self. We had both let go and surrendered; now the dance was dancing us and we were committed to the unconscious communication that had always been there between us.

We cannot *make* the Third Body happen. It comes into being spontaneously yet always exists in the potential space. Paradoxically it is often as a result of an impasse or an enactment (as with Dean) that the therapist is pushed to the edge of or even beyond their comfort zone and defences. It is the dialectical exchange of two subjectivities that gives rise to the Third Body. There is no longer a separate *me* or a *you* but a shared system, an intersubjective third or *We*. There is a oneness about it, yet it is not an undifferentiated pre-egoic merger (see Chapter 1 for more detail of Re-Vision's wheel). There is a differentiation yet at the same time togetherness and intimacy. It has the qualities of space, rhythm, fluidity and freedom.[36]

This Third Body is not just a psychic phenomenon but has its own somatic reality, its own physiology and dynamics. This is the body that therapist and client share yet are independent of it and one another. It does not involve a loss of individuality but includes it in a greater awareness of a differentiated unity (the psyche as whole). There is a movement from the dyad in rhythm through attunement, matching, and mirroring to a rhythmic relational third which emerges out of the two separate rhythms. Just as a physical body has its own intrinsic biological rhythm (breath, heartbeat, circadian rhythm), so this Third Body has its own rhythm too and both parties are influenced by it. It transforms both; it transforms the *whole relationship.*

This Third Body can easily collapse back into a two-body state as it frequently did with Dean. It is not a permanent fixed condition that is arrived at and remains there. We cannot hold on to it. We cannot pinpoint the Third Body. We cannot locate it in time and space because it is not in time and space. It is, as Winnicott said of transitional space, an illusion.[37] It is alive and fluid, it has its own dynamic qualities and character.

Dean and I worked together for a year and a half. He was no longer caught up in fights yet his body was easily triggered and it was at this level that real change had to occur. We worked hard to identify the precise moments when he would adopt a defensive gesture whenever he felt vulnerable and out of control. He knew how quickly this could turn to rage and he no longer wanted that. It was slow, moment by moment work. I would stop him whenever I detected his stress levels rise; and he learned to recognize the signals for himself – a stiffening of his facial muscles, a fixed stare, raising his shoulders, heat rising up his body and then thrusting his whole body forwards. At those times my body would momentarily also revert back to its old defensive postures but I too learned to soothe my fear response and stay connected to Dean in the present.

> *'The young Dean doesn't have to feel out of control any more, not now that the adult Dean is here with him,' I said. 'What would help the young Dean really feel you there protecting him?'*
>
> *'There was a picture of a black lion on the kitchen wall when I was a kid,' he said. 'I used to think he was my friend, I reckoned he could see everything that was going on and he looked out for me. I could think of him.'*
>
> *It felt like we were more together than ever before. There was room to breathe. There was trust, his of me and mine of him. I could take risks. We joked about his choice of animal T-shirts which he agreed always seemed to match his mood.*

I had seen a documentary film of Anna Breytenbach, an interspecies animal communicator with a gift for understanding what animals in the wild and in captivity are communicating.[38] A black leopard called Diabolo had arrived at a rescue centre for wild cats in South Africa. He was vicious and very dangerous. I was reminded of this film when Dean told me about the picture of the black lion. I thought of the wild animal I had seen in Dean's face and body so many times and now had an image of Dean himself as the black lion who saw everything and kept watch.

In the film, Diabolo communicates to Anna about his past maltreatment and concern for two young cubs that he was separated from. The owners of the rescue centre were sceptical about the idea of an animal communicator but it transpired that there were indeed two cubs that Anna did not know of. Anna assured the black leopard that he would not be maltreated here and that the cubs were safe. To acknowledge his arrival in a safe environment and out of respect for this beautiful creature, his name was changed from Diabolo to Spirit. He became a transformed animal, no longer dangerous yet still wild. I suggested Dean watch the film.

Dean's disorganized and chaotic upbringing was reflected in his erratic attendance. I became alarmed when he stopped coming after this session. Some weeks later I finally made contact. He came. I was reluctant to address the non-attendance, worried how he would respond and that we might lose the intersubjective connection. However I knew I had to broach it. Breakdown and repair were an integral part of our work and his healing.

As soon as I mentioned the missed sessions he fixed me with the cold stare again, jutted his chin out and moved his shoulders forwards. This time I moved forwards too and, in order to help Dean feel me alongside and thinking about him, said 'I'm with you Dean. Where were you? I was worried about you and angry when you didn't reply.'

He had gone to an ayahuasca ceremony. He spoke fast, his words were a blur. I wasn't able make sense of what he was saying to begin with but I 'got' that whatever it was it was really important. The drug, he said, had taken him to his 'core'. Under the influence he had heard my voice saying to him 'your anger has a rightful place Dean' and saw the face of a wild black cat staring at him.

After the ceremony and the effects of the drug had worn off, he thought of this black cat and the resemblance to the picture of the black lion on his childhood kitchen wall. He remembered the film I had mentioned and watched it. Everything came together in that moment. He couldn't believe what he was seeing. He cried like never before. How could I possibly have known about the two young cubs? I didn't know what cubs he was talking about. He sobbed as he told me about his two young sons. He was no longer in contact with them for which he blamed himself. I was dumbstruck by the synchronicity.

We had opened into a space of Thirdness, he and I, his body and my body were more than attuned. There was a resonance, an openness between us. And out of this meeting a Third Body emerged. It felt instinctual, erotic and alive. Till this moment I hadn't known of his two children, yet it was as if I did. Was it the effect of the ayahuasca as a Third Body that was having its psychedelic effect on both of us? Or perhaps it was the use of the Internet that had acted as a Third Body? Or my supervisor as a Third Body who so often provided the space for me to reflect about what was going on.

Wherever it came from, in that moment this palpable living Third Body helped our dyadic system move deeper into a place of mutual respect, as if we could mind read one another. Our feelings and intentions were shared. We were together and yet separate. It was without doubt a soulful connection. Not controlled or controlling like before but both surrendering to something that was more spacious and expansive. It was as if a caged wild animal had been freed back into nature, its own nature. We were both there in that moment. An animal that was now free and capable of feeling real love and affection for another. Dean was looking at me intently. There was a recognition of one another that went far deeper than the content of what was said. I noticed his yellow green eyes again, they were uncannily similar to those of the black leopard Spirit I had seen on the film. I was in touch with a sense of awe and wonder at Dean's power and magnificence. It was as if in that moment I had become the animal communicator Anna and he, now, the beautiful and majestic Spirit.

Concluding Thoughts

Writing this chapter has put me in touch with the very intimate nature of psychotherapy especially when working relationally and from a soulful perspective. Dean and I shared the same air or, as Bly says in the opening verse, our breaths together fed someone whom we did not know. Nick Totton says of the therapist, 'Our body bathes in and soaks up the embodied presence of the client; we catch fire from her; we *breathe* (my italics) her in and metabolise her; our ground state reverberates to her rhythms, and our own rhythms shift to meet them'.[39] I suggest that in the space of thirdness this is a reciprocal phenomenon. There were many moments of authentic meeting between Dean and myself, none of which I would have believed possible when we first met. By the time we ended our work there was a profound sense of respect for the other. What was it that shifted the interactive regulation from one of control to one of co-operation? What was it that enabled this powerful transformation for both of us to occur?

Dean's aggressive and intimidating behaviour suggested a history of not having been well cared for early in life. In the face of the violence he had experienced, a sympathetically activated fighting response was his best coping strategy. His ability to self regulate was poor, he had poor impulse control, and he lived with chronic levels of stress. On the other hand Dean had strong moral principles in line with Graham Music's observation of children with reactive aggressive styles.[40] The fights he got in typically were triggered by a perceived injustice aimed either at himself or someone else. Just as Spirit was concerned for the welfare of two cubs, so Dean showed concern for others less able to defend themselves. Whilst the extent to which he was genuinely able to empathize was questionable, given the lack of early attunement and sensitivity shown towards him as a child, as he became more able to regulate his emotions and feel better about himself so he became more open and trusting. Sharing his muffins was a sign of a growing capacity for mentalization. By the time he was able to feel and express the pain of separation from his own children, Dean was in touch with real feelings of grief, love and compassion.

I showed Dean the proof of this chapter for his permission to go to print. After he finished reading it he chuckled 'That's really good!' It was said with an air of accomplishment and deep satisfaction. I took his comment to mean that our work together and the healing he found for himself to have been 'really good'. As he handed the draft back, I caught a brief glimpse of Voluptas in the room, smiling.

I am a great believer in the life-changing benefits of Winnicott's facilitating environment.[41] In my work with Dean I endeavoured to create a space with good enough secure holding for the emotionally deprived young Dean. Dean was at heart a moral individual. Research and evidence shows that we have an innate capacity to be prosocial, altruistic, cooperative and generous.[42] This is not to say that genes do not have a role, but experience shapes our brains, our sense of self and our relationship to the world. Given a supportive environment and neuroplasticity, new neural pathways and prosocial qualities and behaviour can grow throughout our lifespan.

The nature of the intersubjective field between Dean and myself changed and evolved over time from a strong feeling of separateness to one of togetherness, some might say even telepathy. How was the communication between us happening? Freud's famous statement that 'It is a very remarkable thing that the Unconscious of one human being can react upon that of another, without passing through the Conscious' speaks to me of the remarkable mystery of soul.[43] Some of what was occurring we can explain in terms of unconscious communication, or neurobiology and autonomic interactive regulation, subtle nonverbal cues, complex brain processes and so forth, but I suggest that alongside all of these there is a point at which psyche and soma meet in a space between that is neither material nor immaterial but both. Beyond the two (separate) subjectivities a shared field that both individuals occupy has its own vitality and is the Third Body. I suggest that the Third Body exists at all times where two individuals are in dialogue, whether it be conscious or unconscious, realized/emergent or in potential, and that this third area comes into awareness at specific moments in the therapeutic process. If the therapist can allow their own woundedness, or as Schwartz-Salant describes it 'the waters of madness', then the mystery of the Third Body becomes more possible.[44]

[1] Robert Bly, 'A Third Body', in *Loving a Woman in Two Worlds* (London: Harper & Row, 1985), p. 19.

[2] Maurice Merleau-Ponty, *The Phenomenology of Perception* (London: Routledge & Kegan Paul, 1962), p. 216.

[3] Roberto Assagioli, *Psychosynthesis: A Collection of Basic Writings* (Wellingborough: Turnstone Books, 1965), p. 123.

[4] James Hillman, *Myth Of Analysis: Three Essays in Archetypal Psychology* (Evanston, IL: Northwestern University Press, 1972), p. 51.

[5] James Hillman, *Re-visioning Psychology* (New York: Harper & Row, 1975), p. xvi.

[6] Novalis, *Vermischte Bemerkingen* (Various Remarks, II, 1797) p. 418, 20.

[7] Murray Stein, 'The Interactive Field as the Analytic Object', in *The Interactive Field in Analysis*, Vol. 1 (Wilmette, IL: Chiron Publications, 1995).

[8] Donald W. Winnicott, 'Transitional Objects and Transitional Phenomena A Study of the First Not-Me Possession', *International Journal of Psychoanalysis* 34 (1953), pp. 89 – 97.

[9] Stein, 'The Interactive Field', p. 5.

[10] Allan Schore, *Affect Regulation and Repair of the Self* (New York and London: Norton, 2003), p. 80.

[11] Schore, *Affect Regulation*, p. 98.

[12] Lewis Aron, 'Analytic impasse and the third: Clinical implications of intersubjectivity theory', *International Journal of Psychoanalysis* 87, no. 2 (2006), pp. 349 – 368.

[13] Stephen Mitchell, *Influence and Autonomy in Psychoanalysis* (Hillsdale, NJ: Analytic Press, 1997).

[14] Robert D. Stolorow and George E. Atwood, 'The Intersubjective Perspective', *Psychoanalytic Review* 83 (1996), pp. 181 – 194.

[15] Jessica Benjamin, 'Beyond Doer and Done To: An Intersubjective View Of Thirdness', *Psychoanalytic Quarterly* 73 (2004), pp. 5 – 46.

[16] Nick Totton, *Embodied Relating* (London: Karnac, 2015), p. 48.

[17] Stephen Mitchell, *Relationality: From Attachment to Intersubjectivity* (Hillsdale, NJ: Analytic Press, 2000).

[18] Carl G. Jung, *The Practice of Psychotherapy, Collected Works*, Vol. 16, 2nd edn (London: Routledge & Kegan Paul, 1966), para. 163.

[19] Carl G. Jung, *The Practice of Psychotherapy*, para. 166.

[20] Wilfred R. Bion, *Second Thoughts: Selected Papers on Psycho-Analysis* (New York: Jason Aronson, 1967).

[21] Donald W. Winnicott, *Playing and Reality* (London: Routledge, 1991).

[22] Thomas H. Ogden, 'On potential space', *International Journal of Psychoanalysis* 66 (1985), pp. 129 – 142.

[23] Jessica Benjamin, *Beyond Doer and Done To: Recognition Theory, Intersubjectivity and the Third* (London and New York: Routledge, 2018).

[24] Jacques Lacan, 'The Psychoanalytic Act', in *The Seminar of Jacques Lacan*, XV/1–19, 27.03.1968, at http://www.lacaninireland.com/web/wp-content/uploads/2010/06/Book-15-The-Psychoanalytical-Act.pdf (accessed 23 May 2018).

[25] Carl G. Jung, *The Practice of Psychotherapy*, p. 8.

[26] Adrienne Harris and Kathy Sinsheimer, 'The Analyst's Vulnerability', in Frances Sommer Anderson, ed., *Bodies in Treatment: The Unspoken Dimension* (New York and London: Analytic Press, 2008), p. 259.

[27] Louis Cozolino, *The Neuroscience of Human Relationships: Attachment and the Developing Brain* (New York: W. W. Norton & Company, Inc., 2006).

[28] Thomas Moore, *Sex and the Soul* (New York: Harper Collins, 1998).

[29] Erich Neumann, *Amor and Psyche: The Psychic Development of the Feminine: A Commentary on the Tale by Apuleius* (Princeton, NJ: Princeton University Press, 1956), p. 92.

[30] Carl G. Jung, *The Psychology of the Transference, Collected Works*, Vol. 16, 3rd edn (Princeton, NJ: Princeton University Press, 1974), para. 399; Winnicott, *Playing and Reality*, p. 107; Thomas H. Ogden, 'The Analytic Third: Working with Intersubjective Clinical Facts', *International Journal of Psychoanalysis* 75 (1994), pp. 3 – 19; and Jessica Benjamin, 'Beyond Doer and Done To'.

[31] Jane Burka, 'The therapist's body in reality and fantasy: a perspective from an overweight therapist', in *The Therapist as a Person*, ed. B. Gerson (Hillside, NJ: Analytic Press, 1996), pp. 255 – 275.

[32] Thomas Ogden, 'The Analytic Third', p. 4.

[33] Roz Carroll, 'Self-regulation: an evolving concept at the heart of body psychotherapy', in L. Hartley, ed., *Contemporary Body Psychotherapy: The Chiron Approach* (London: Routledge, 2009), pp. 89 – 105, citing Beatrice Beebe and Frank Lachmann, *Infant Research and Adult Treatment: Co-constructing Interactions* (Hillsdale, NJ: Analytic Press, 2002).

[34] Susan Sands, 'Self Psychology and Projective Identification', *Psychoanalytic Dialogues 7* (1997), p. 653.

[35] Jessica Benjamin, *Beyond Doer and Done To*, p. 39.

[36] Jessica Benjamin, *Beyond Doer and Done To*.

[37] Winnicott, *Playing and Reality*.

[38] *The Incredible Story of How Leopard Diabolo Became Spirit*, at https://www.youtube.com/watch?v=gvwHHMEDdTo Full length documentary film directed by Craig Foster available on DVD.

[39] Nick Totton, *Embodied Relating*, p. 48.

[40] Graham Music, *The Good Life: Wellbeing And The New Science Of Altruism, Selfishness And Immorality* (London and New York: Routledge, 2014).

[41] Donald W. Winnicott, *The Maturational Processes and the Facilitating Environment* (London: Routledge, 1965).

[42] Graham Music, *The Good Life*.

[43] Sigmund Freud, 'The Unconscious', *Standard Edition* 12 (London: Hogarth Press, 1915) p. 126.

[44] Nathan Schwartz Salant, *The Mystery of Human Relationship: Alchemy and the Transformation of the Self* (London: Routledge, 1998), p. 37.

Chapter 4

The Garden of Love
Sarah Van Gogh

> Anyone who wants to know the human psyche will learn next to nothing from experimental psychology. He would be better advised to put away his scholar's gown, bid farewell to his study, and wander with human heart through the world... through love and hate, through the experience of passion in every form in his own body, he would reap richer stores of knowledge than text books a foot thick could give him, and he will know how to doctor the sick with real knowledge of the human soul.[1]

If a therapy training is to give its practitioners the kind of basis that Jung described in his famous essay – one that will enable them to attend deeply to the psychological and emotional wounds of those who come to them for help – then it cannot be a predominantly intellectual exercise. Yet it must not throw the baby of reflection out along with the bathwater of an over-reliance on thinking.

The Re-Vision trainings encourage and foster the capacity to trust being deeply open to the lived, embodied experience of any moment, alongside an ability to reflect and wonder about an experience and the different meanings to be made of it. Re-Vision teaches a craft that that requires practitioners to integrate a developmental and transpersonal lens, through which they can *look again* at any aspect of life. It aims to equip counsellors and psychotherapists with the ability to value both knowing and not-knowing, and give them the capacity to come up with possible notions as to what might ail a person, a relationship, a family, a community, or even our planet. It also gives them ways to feel supported as they travel on the ways of not-yet-knowing, not-yet-understanding, and tolerate the uncertainty that the ego and the rational mind can find so threatening. The trainings are designed to prepare a practitioner to be able to, in effect, wander in the inner realms of experience, rather in the way that an explorer might wander in the outer realms of the world.

Bill Plotkin, psychologist and wilderness guide, describes the four qualities that someone capable of wild wandering must have:

> First, he must in fact be lost. Second, he must know he is lost and accept it. Third, he must have adequate survival knowledge, skills, and physical and spiritual tools. Fourth, and most important, he must... accept his condition, relax into it, and arrive fully where he is.[2]

It is a challenge for the one who is 'supposed' to be the guide – the one who knows, the one who can help – to stay close to the inevitable fact that there will be times when the therapist is lost, that is to say, when they cannot perfectly know, understand, and lead the way. Indeed, that it will be vital to the process that they can acknowledge that they often absolutely do not know best, and cannot be sure of the way the therapy will unfold. For it is only when a therapist can be somewhat lost in the work and know it – can bear and fully accept the fact of being lost, realizing that this is inevitable during genuine exploration – that they can be in touch with something larger and deeper than simply knowing the way. This 'something deeper' is needed if the therapy is to be about more than tweaking some symptoms so that a client can fit in better with some generally agreed social structures. The qualities of soul are needed in therapy that works at depth and is transformational. The soul, as Hillman reminds us, does not soar like spirit, is not heroic, cannot see clearly, does not let the arrow fly; rather, it is quieter, more fumbling, takes the hit of the arrow, and is often associated with whatever the dominant paradigm wants to see as inferior, less worthy, even shameful.[3]

A crucial factor in supporting the therapist to bear with the soulful uncertainty involved in being prepared to not-know and the accompanying anxiety, is for them to know a deep kind of love: love of the work, love in the work, and love of their whole self – broken, wounded and flawed as that self will be. The truly useful therapist seems to need to feel the world as beloved, and to sense that they, and all beings, have their tiny but unique place in it as an integral part of the beloved-ness.

As John Ryan Haule puts it, 'the ethical task of the love-cure therapist is short on certainties and long on doubt. Even the metaphor of the ship's navigator is overly precise. For the love cure sets sail on uncharted waters... '[4]

The following is a fictionalized account of a piece of work that aims to give a flavour of how a therapist who is held lovingly in their own struggles – both by past trainers and in current supervision – might be able to draw on both a developmental and transpersonal perspective as they work, and tolerate working in ways that require a willingness to accompany the client into areas that are uncomfortable and anxiety-provoking for both parties. I have made up Eric and the story of his therapy, drawing on real experiences of my work with many clients over many years, which I have fictionalized. However, I have *not* made up the experience I describe of how a senior colleague once reached out to me, over twenty-five years ago, and profoundly shaped my development as a therapist, all in a moment.

When Eric first arrived for an assessment session, I felt as if an injured, panicky bird had somehow been blown into my room, and I would have to be very careful not to make some slight movement that would send it careering around the place, hurting itself further. He strode in – a tall, gangly, middle aged white guy, swathed in layers of dark clothes and a long scarf, and perched anxiously on the very edge of the seat I showed him to. With his shoulder-length grey hair and long, slightly hooked nose, he looked hawkish as he stared around at his surroundings with rather jerky, nervous movements of his head. He immediately told me in great detail a lot of what was bothering him. This included his long standing alcohol addiction and bulimia, and his various health problems to do with his digestive system. He was straight and, although he very much wanted an intimate relationship with a woman, he found such relationships impossible to maintain and, now in his mid forties, he was single, lonely and sexually frustrated.

He began to tell me, at length, about all the various healing and therapeutic approaches he had experimented with over the years. These included Reiki, astrology, crystal healing, using tarot cards, and taking part in rebirthing rituals. I was struck by how there seemed to be an emphasis on the intuitive and non-rational in the sorts of therapeutic help Eric had sought out so far. These would have fed his hunger for the *feeling* part of his life to be attended to, but might not have addressed the need for this feeling part to work alongside and be supported by the part that can *think* about emotions, sensations and feelings. Without that capacity, he was able to only have powerful, cathartic experiences during his efforts to heal, with no way of then anchoring them into a meaningful context. T. S. Eliot refers to this in *Four Quartets*: 'We had the experience but missed the meaning'.[5]

After a lot of detail about all of his previous therapeutic endeavours, and what they had and hadn't been able to do for him, I said I would like to interrupt him in order to ask something.

> **Sarah:** *'It sounds as if you have done such a lot of work already, and come to some very important insights for yourself. I want to ask if you know what you'd hope to get out of coming here, to see me for some therapy sessions?'*

Eric looked suddenly non-plussed at being interrupted. The agitation he had shown on entering the room, which had lessened as he had been telling me about his previous therapeutic work, came back. And then he did something he was to do often in our work together, when his inner process lay 'too deep for tears'.[6] He seemed to be able to call on some ability to reach out instinctively into the physical environment in order to find something in that environment which could convey to me something about his inner landscape, which he could not do by himself, in his own words.

He turned his head and scanned the nearby bookshelves, and then swiftly reached out an arm to pull one book down. It was a facsimile copy of William Blake's *Songs of Innocence & Experience*.[7] He began to leaf through it, sometimes with a frown of concentration, and sometimes with an excited smile, muttering to him-

self, 'Yes, yes... That's it, that's quite right. Yup. He's got it, there.'
Whatever was going on as he looked through the book seemed to
be pleasurably meaningful for him. Then he came to a stop on one
page and read and re-read the poem on it. First he read it quickly,
speaking the words rapidly under his breath, but then he slowed
down, re-read it and began to say the lines out loud more clearly,
until he spoke the final lines in a pained tone that rose higher and
higher until it collapsed into a sob. He threw the book down at his
feet when he had finished, looked up at me and said through his
tears, 'Well, there you go!' The poem was 'The Garden of Love'.

I went to the Garden of Love
And saw what I never had seen:
A chapel was built in the midst,
Where I used to play on the green.

And the gates of this Chapel were shut,
And 'Thou shalt not' writ over the door;
so I turned to the Garden of Love,
That so many sweet flowers bore,

And I saw it was filled with graves
and tomb-stones where flowers should be;
And priests in black gowns were walking their rounds,
And binding with briars my joys and desires.

I noticed that I felt a strong sensation in my chest as Eric read
the poem and then wept. I tried to think about this sensation as I
felt it. It was as if a number of strings, rather like those on a violin,
had somehow formed in the air between us, and they were becoming attached, at one end, to my heart, and at the other, to somewhere within Eric. The poem's words, as Eric spoke them, seemed
to create a force that gently but insistently plucked on these
strings, which was exquisitely uncomfortable and compelling. I
found the phrase 'to tug at the heartstrings' coming to my mind.
All this helped me to feel clearer about what depth of pain and anguish there might be in Eric's inner landscape; about how much
he was longing for a kind of acceptance within a relationship,

which his overtly mystical and spiritual searching had not yet provided; and also about the potential there clearly was for me to be open-hearted enough to Eric and his story for us to form the kind of attachment and alliance that is the bedrock of therapeutic work.

There was a silence for a while as Eric wept noisily, which eventually slowed to a calmer crying, and finally stopped. He drew a deep, quivering breath, wiped his face, and dropped a ball of tissues in the nearby wastepaper bin.

> **Sarah:** *'I'm glad you found that poem to read. It seems to have really touched you. And it's very helpful for me to hear, in the form of a metaphor, what you would still like help with. Something along the lines of – you want some more help in untangling some of the briars that 'bind up your joys and desires'?'*
>
> **Eric:** (Through the last of his tears) *'Yes, that's very good. Very good way of putting it, old William B has.'*

By the end of the session we had established a number of key things, including that Eric had well-paid, part-time work in IT, a supportive manager who knew about him coming to counselling to help with his drinking problem, that he was not suicidal, and was keen to come to a further six sessions, after which we would review how helpful he was finding the process. From then on, for the next three years, Eric attended weekly counselling sessions faithfully. He never missed an appointment, and very gradually, showed a great number of improvements in his capacity to care for himself, manage his alcohol intake, and have more positive, rewarding relationships in his life.

His history helped us to see his many emotional and psychological difficulties in a larger context. The therapy helped Eric in a way his other attempts at healing had not, in terms of helping him to *think about* and *feel into* how the seeds for much of his troubling behaviour had been planted in his early childhood. He was the youngest of four boys, brought up in the North of England by a mother who had been a nurse and a father who had worked in engineering, and who were both devout fundamentalist Christians and strict disciplinarians. His parents had had harsh, unloving up-bringings themselves, which had left them with little patience for anything that they had decided was not 'right and normal.' They had both displayed a sadistic relish in enforcing their boys' 'good' behaviour. Their father kept an old leather belt in the coat cupboard, and whichever boy was to be punished had to fetch the belt, summon any of his brothers in the house at the time to the kitchen, go there himself, drop his trousers and underwear, and be beaten by their dad in front of his siblings, which was deeply humiliating as well as frightening and painful.

Eric had, by the sounds of it, been a dreamy, rather artistic little boy who could easily transgress because his mind had wandered or because he had felt an urge to experiment or create something a bit out of the ordinary. This was usually followed by a beating from his father, or another punishment, meted out by his mother, which would, as Eric said, 'fit the crime'. Once, when his mother had found that he had drawn with an orange crayon on his bedroom wall, aged about six, she had made him eat it, sitting with him on his bed to ensure he chewed and swallowed the whole, large crayon, even though he was choking and crying as he did so. After this, not surprisingly, Eric began to have symptoms of a 'sensitive stomach' and digestive problems, for which he was often dosed with unpleasant medicines or given enemas. As Eric described this incident I noticed that the strings between us were being added to. I not only felt my heart being tugged at the thought of that small boy being forced to eat a crayon, but I could also imagine some new strings had appeared between us, some of which had now attached themselves into my guts and some into my throat. I was aware of a painful twisting as the strings seemed to pull at my stomach, and my guts became knotted in a mirroring of the cramping and discomfort I imagined Eric had felt. I was also aware of my throat becoming hot and tight as a sour taste arose in my mouth. It seemed the strings between us were vibrating and passing on to me some aspects of the disturbance and pain that Eric had experienced as he choked down the crayon, and which he regularly endured as an adult, during the dreadfully debilitating episodes he had when his Irritable Bowel Syndrome (IBS) flared up.

There was one especially bitter moment from Eric's earlier life to which he returned in sessions, a number of times. He was around fourteen and had written his mother a series of poems for Mother's Day, as a gift to her. He left them on her bed, and then had waited on tenterhooks for her response, only to find them, that evening, placed back on his bed, with no word or acknowledgement from his mother. He had felt eaten up by a mixture of anger and hurt for months after this. Some years later, around the age of eighteen, he had raised the matter with his mother and asked her why she had just given them back. She had dismissed the episode as 'just more of your nonsense', and had said it had seemed obvious to her that, as she knew nothing about poetry, it made sense to just have a quick look at the poems, and when she could see they 'weren't up to much, because they didn't even rhyme', to simply return them.

It became obvious to me that a key part of what helped Eric feel he could trust the work we were engaged in, and could tolerate my invitations to wonder about what impact some of his early experiences might have had on him, was because I had lots of poetry books on my shelves, and that I had explicitly made clear to him that I thought poetry and metaphors were useful and worthwhile. Reading and writing poetry had always been important to me and had helped me to feel loved throughout my life. It seems that Eric, also a poet and lover of poetry, and I were being held, together and lovingly, by Poetry herself, in the work. This allowed for a deep mutual understanding and appreciation of each other that did not need to be spoken, but which simply and quietly fostered the building of our alliance and its capacity to weather the storms of what would inevitably threaten that alliance.

The therapy proceeded smoothly enough for about two years and then things began to change. There was a particularly difficult period of about six months when Eric, having been a model client in terms of time-keeping and not drinking before sessions, began to challenge the boundaries of the work very intensely. In supervision we discussed the fact that these boundary challenges seemed to spike in their intensity and frequency directly after he had told me that our sessions were helping him a lot, 'because you never criticize me or tell me what to do'. It seemed that after a ges-

74

tation period of 'good enough' containment, Eric felt able and willing to test my boundaries in order to see how authentic my capacity to hold him really was. This most testing time for us reached a climax in one session. This same session also proved to be a turning point in Eric's healing.

Eric arrived late, which was unusual for him. He had been steadily behaving in more and more eccentric ways over the past month, including arriving one time with a handful of berries he had picked from my neighbours' gardens as a gift for me. He was also spending a lot of time in the week, he told me, walking through central London, on the hunt for the scores of gold rings he was convinced were being dropped carelessly on the streets. However, he was still going to work, still coming to sessions on time, and still having some days when he didn't drink heavily.

I discussed Eric's increasing eccentricity with my supervisor periodically. After he had described his daily hunts for dropped gold rings, I talked with her about my concern that Eric might be floating away towards the more psychotic end of the spectrum of disturbance, and that he was becoming delusional. I told her I feared that I was reaching the edge of what I could help Eric with, as a therapist, and that it might be more appropriate if I suggested to Eric that he speak with his GP about having a psychiatric assessment. She was of the view that the strong alliance that Eric and I had formed was crucial and should not be disturbed. She encouraged me to believe that the therapy was giving Eric the safety to contact some very disturbing feelings that he was gradually going to be able to think about in non-delusional ways, if he continued to receive the warmth and support of his relationship with me. She held the possibility that the safety of the sessions was allowing his deeper pathology to emerge and be worked with, when I was not so sure. As long as Eric felt he could rely on the bridging nature of therapy, she suggested, he would eventually be able to translate what he was currently seeing as actual fact (dropped gold rings) into metaphor – something that connects ideas to emotions. She trusted he still had the capacity to make meaning out of this idea that he had of gold rings being dropped in London, and encouraged me to experiment with doing the same.

She asked me, 'What comes to you if you just wonder aloud, in supervision right now, about the possible meaning of many gold rings being dropped on busy streets? Just free associate!' I opened my mouth to see what would come out, and found myself saying, 'Precious objects, often symbolizing a sacred bond, being carelessly cast aside.'

Immediately, I could feel a wave of clarity and pity swell up in me as I pondered this. Perhaps Eric was trying to communicate to himself and to me how repeatedly the beautiful 'gold ring' of his love for and fidelity to (or, developmentally speaking, his attachment) to his mother and father had been carelessly dropped by them.

The fact that it was on London streets that Eric thought the rings had been dropped, might also point to something I had not fully been contacting thus far in the work, which was to do with me imagining something about the inner experiences of Eric's parents. London streets evoke hectically busy, day to day, commercial affairs. When he was young, Eric's parents had been working flat-out in demanding, practical jobs, to provide for themselves and their boys. Tragically, as they did so, they were dropping the golden rings of the love between a parent and child, all unawares. I could suddenly contact more compassion and empathy for them, as I let myself feel a sorrow on their behalf at all they had missed because of feeling under such endless financial pressure and hardship.

When I amplified Eric's story of dropped golden rings in this way, I noticed my anxiety level about whether or not I could be of use to him decrease dramatically. It was an absolute gift of a metaphor, both for how Eric had experienced his parents' attitude to him when he was young, and for how they had felt as they worked away at their jobs. He was offering it to me. And I had so nearly missed its value and dropped it, just as his mother had tended to do with his subtle, creative offerings!

So his idea of wanting to find dropped gold rings was not mad at all, seen in one way, but was, instead, rather brilliantly sane. How fitting that of all the poets on my shelf, at the first session, Eric had picked out William Blake – now recognized as uniquely gifted, and at the time, often thought of as quite mad.

One day, a few weeks after this helpful supervision, Eric looked terribly unwell when I opened the door to him: he had a greyish complexion, very wild hair, an unwashed appearance and a strong smell of alcohol around him. He immediately announced, before I had even fully opened the door, 'I've been drinking all week! I stopped last night because of coming to counselling...' adding in a desperate tone, 'Can I still come in?' He did not look as if he was actually drunk, so I agreed. Once he sat down he looked more than usually restless. He looked around the room, cleared his throat, leaned back and said, as if to the ceiling, 'You'll know this... I mean, I thought you would probably know this: I was wondering all night long what the........ you know... the name.... the name of that....the...the... you know, the star is. You know, the one you can navigate by? The.... the, the proper name for the North Star. You know? Because I've been navigating, I mean, meditating all night on it, but then I thought, I really ought to be using the, you know, the proper terminology. Its proper name. Do you know it?'

> **Sarah:** 'You're hoping I'll know the Latin or Greek name for the North Star?'
> **Eric:** 'Yes. That's it. I thought you'd know.' (He sat up and stared at me worriedly.) 'Is that a bit mad?'
> **Sarah:** 'I don't think wanting to know the name of some-thing is necessarily mad. I wonder if you are worried about feeling mad?'
> **Eric:** (with a sigh) 'No, no. I know I'm not mad. I just didn't want you to think I am. I thought you'd know the name. That's all.'

Madness is a loaded word. Sometimes, when I was working with Eric, I *did* feel worried that he was veering further and further away from a path on which I could follow or be any of use to him. At such times, I would often, after a session, find myself thinking of some of my favourite therapy ancestors – Jung, Winnicott, R. D. Laing – who had kept faith with their profoundly psychotic patients, trusting that there was a kind of deep sanity in what they were saying and doing, if it could be listened to with the ear of compassion and imaginative understanding. In this session, after a pause, I found myself doing what Eric often did when he was at a loss for words – I turned to look at my bookshelves.

If, as Balint has it in *The Basic Fault*, '... it is an idle question to ask if the water in a fish's gills is part of the fish or part of the ocean...', then perhaps it is equally fruitless to wonder, in hindsight, exactly how to explain what drew me to imitate Eric at this moment, by looking to my bookshelves for help.[8] One book seemed to leap out at me as I did so: a large, A3-size star atlas that had been given as a present to one of my sons.

> **Sarah:** *'I wonder if this book would show us.'*

I took it down and placed it on the floor between us and turned some pages. Eric leaned forward with great interest and after a few moments I sat back, and Eric began to leaf through it eagerly, by himself. There was page after page of detailed images of different portions of the night sky. It seemed as if it might be like looking for a needle in a haystack to try and find one star in the many thousands on display.

I had never looked in the book before, and after a while Eric and I both became caught up in simply marvelling together at the beautiful and awe-inspiring representations of the cosmos. It could be that it was a relief for both of us, in those moments, to have the opportunity to psychically wander in something so common to all beings – something so wordless, so vast, and so full of new things to discover as space.

After a few minutes of page turning and the occasional murmur of surprise or admiration from each of us, the name 'Polaris' popped into my mind.

> **Sarah:** *'Is the North Star also know as 'Polaris'? I asked, tentatively.*
>
> *And almost immediately, Eric placed a forefinger emphatically on a page, right where the North Star was, and announced, 'Yes! And there it is!' He sat back with a triumphant smile.*
>
> **Sarah:** *'Oh! You found it!'*
>
> **Eric:** *'Yup. We did it. That's the name I wanted.' He re-*

laxed visibly in the chair and closed his eyes. There was a long silence.

I felt a frisson at the rather uncanny nature of what had just happened. Eric and I could have been looking at any page of many in that book, and at any place on that page crowded with stars. Yet the exact moment that the name of the guiding star had come into my mind, was the very same one in which Eric had finally spotted it in one tiny place in the book's representation of the cosmos. I sat there, wondering, and feeling at the affect of such synchrony: Eric and I had suddenly been given an opportunity to be aware of and feel something of the wider field in which our relationship was being conducted.

This moment could be understood through the lens of the Re-Vision 'wheel' that distinguishes between the experiences of :1) pre-ego, 2) ego, and 3) trans-ego states.

- Eric and I were not in the merged, **pre-ego** state of actually blending together ('There is no **me** and no **you**, but only an **us**'). This was in part due to the fact that I had enough ego strength to have the equivalent of Plotkin's 'adequate survival knowledge, skills, and physical and spiritual tools.' (See note 2) and partly because Eric's own ego strength had been slowly growing during the work.

- For much of the work to date, Eric and I had needed to relate in the realm of the **ego** ('I am me and The Other is distinct from me') in order to help him build up more of a personal boundary that would not leave him so very permeable and super-vulnerable in the world.

- But the synchronous moment that arose from us looking together at the book on astronomy had allowed a glimpse of another way that we were in relationship, and made it possible for us to be more aware that he and I were also connected in a way that includes and yet is beyond the personal. Rather than feeling that we were two ego-encapsulated beings, we instead found ourselves inhabiting a liminal space, the space in which Buber's 'I-Thou' relationship with The Other is possible, alongside feeling a connection to the wider world in which the 'I-Thou' relationship is happening. ('You and I are intimately connected, both to each other and to the great Web of Being').[9]

I noticed I felt a kind of gratitude as we sat in silence. I felt as if we had just been generously helped, in a way that had been totally unexpected and out of my hands. The image of golden rings came back to my memory, and I wondered if this was because, in that moment, Eric may have felt that he had at last, metaphorically speaking, found one of those treasured rings: had finally and consciously felt a deep sense of attachment and belonging, both to me and the wider world.

> *Sarah:* 'Perhaps it feels very important to remember the name of the star that can be used to work out where you are. It's comforting to think about a thing that can be used to get your bearings anywhere in the universe.'
>
> *Eric opened his eyes and smiled weakly at me. He looked quite exhausted.* 'Yes. I think that's about right.' *He looked down at the book, and said wistfully,* 'It's a lovely thing. You must know a lot about the stars.'
>
> *Sarah:* 'Well, I don't know as much as the people involved in making this book.'
>
> *Eric:* 'No. That would almost be too much. Amazing, really. How do they find it all out?' *He leaned forward and began turning the pages again. After half a dozen turns, he began to spend less and less time looking at the pages, and turned each one faster and faster until, I noticed with an inner wince of displeasure, that he had turned one page so fast he made a slight rip in the bottom corner. He stopped and studied this page, apparently oblivious to the damage he had caused.*

All of a sudden I felt a disturbing flare of hot, blaming anger rise up in my chest and throat. I could detect a sudden strong urge in me to draw Eric's attention to what he had just done, and make him 'the bad one' in the situation. I was also aware that I felt a painful twinge of guilt and shame – I had not asked my son's permission to use his book in my work sessions, and now it was damaged! My anger with Eric had a flavour of 'Why couldn't he have been more careful with a book I had been generous enough to share with him? Now I am going to have to be exposed in my piece of poor judgement, and own up to my son that I used his book without asking him!' So as well as angry, I felt a fool.

But it had been wholly my decision to offer the book to Eric, knowing full well, as I did, that he was prone to little accidents. I was well aware that he quite often spilled his glass of water in the session, or knocked over the box of tissues, or tripped over my rug in the hall. So where had this sudden fierce urge in me come from – to angrily blame him entirely for another mishap? I managed, figuratively, to catch the coat tails of this urge quickly enough to prevent me from obviously conveying my annoyance to Eric. I managed, instead, to stay quiet, which gave me to time wonder if my feelings could be understood as a mixture of both *complementary countertransference*, which gave me a clue as to how Eric's mother may have responded when he made similar mistakes and errors as a boy; and *concordant countertransference*, which gave me a flavour of how foolish and exposed Eric himself felt when he was confronted with the fact he had made a mistake.

When he looked up I could see he now had a stricken expression on his face. His cheeks and throat had suddenly flushed a deep red. (Perhaps his rush of blood to that area was mirroring my own). He looked down and said quickly,

> **Eric:** *'Oh, um, sorry. I think I might have torn it. Did I? No. Or.... was that there before? I don't think it was. Sorry. Well, I didn't mean to.'* (He cleared his throat with an angry-sounding cough and glanced up at me).
> *My ability to wonder if I had momentarily embodied his mother's reaction to any of Eric's wrong doings, along with*

the unmistakeable fear on his face, quickly dissolved my own blaming anger and embarrassment; I could see a frightened, vulnerable child looking at me out of Eric's face.

Sarah: (Gently, firmly) *'If you did, I know that you that you didn't mean to, Eric.'*

He sat back and clasped his hands tightly in his lap, and said in a low, rather strangled tone, 'I don't think I'd better look at it any more.'

I picked the book up and put it to one side on a nearby low table.

Sarah: *'I think a small tear like that can be taped up quite easily.'*

Eric: (Sounding doubtful) *'Really?'*

Sarah: *'Yes. I think it will be OK. And, you know, that little tear has made me think of something about your childhood.'*

Eric: *'Has it?'* (The flushing on his cheeks and throat began to die away as he spoke. My anger and embarrassment were dissipating too). *'That's funny, because it's reminded me of the sort of stuff I'd get into trouble for back then, too.'*

Sarah: *'The sorts of small accidents you would be punished quite severely for?'*

Eric: (with a sudden grimace) *'Yes.'* He started to breathe quite heavily, and shift around in his seat.

I took a little risk at this point, hoping that I would be pushing gently at a door that was already opening.

Sarah: *'The sorts of harsh punishments that were unfair to a little boy who kept trying to please his parents, but just couldn't seem to get it right for them?'*

The effect of this comment on Eric was more potent than I had reckoned on. He let out a whimper, nodded, and then hunched over as if his stomach suddenly hurt him terribly. He began to gasp and sob, and rocked back and forth with his arms folded over his stomach.

Sarah: *'I can see you're suddenly feeling such a lot of distress. It looks so painful.'*

Eric: (Through little gasps and sudden copious tears)

'I'm thinking....I'm thinking of those times, those times......You know, one time I was downstairs and my mother shouted so loud at one of my brothers upstairs - not even at me, but at Joe – and I was still so scared..... I dropped all my sweets, and......and .... and (in an anguished whisper) *they all got spoiled.'*

Although it was clearly so painful for Eric to connect to and articulate this memory, and – to a lesser extent – for me to hear about it, it was a hopeful indication that, in this moment, he was capable of the integrating and healing capacity to have his cognitive functioning and affect regulation working together.

He sobbed quietly, and then thumped the arm of his chair and shouted so suddenly and loudly that it made me jump slightly.

Eric: *'That bitch! I hate her! I hate her for scaring us all to death. No need! There was no need at all. She stabbed me in the heart, when all I wanted for her was to give me a little bit of affection. God, I hate her guts!'*

It is important to name that at no time did I feel frightened for myself during this session. I felt no threat from Eric, although he was so angry and upset; it was clear that he had a good awareness about the person with whom he was very angry, i.e., his mother, and he was angry about the behaviour she had displayed when he had been a child. I imagine that he had been helped not to confuse me with the mother of his childhood precisely because I had managed to have a different reaction to his small transgression from the reaction his mother had tended to have when he was small and had made mistakes. I had, in effect been able to process (i.e. stay present to and digest) the sorts of horribly difficult sensations that Eric's mother had been unable to whenever her small son transgressed; this meant she had also been unable to teach him how to stay present to and bear his own sensations, when he was angry or upset.

Sarah: *'You feel so angry on behalf of the little boy you were, who longed for more of his mother's love and approval.'*

Eric continued to rock and weep in a high, keening tone. When his sobs began to lessen, he remained hunched over, but in a slightly more open posture, with his hands over his face to begin with; then, once he had finished sobbing, he let both arms hang limply down at his sides. There was now a long silence that felt to me potentially fruitful. Different expressions flitted across Eric's face, as something seemed to be getting processed internally. A sense of grief and compassion for the child that he had once been was palpable between us in the room.

After a while he surprised me again. He looked up at my face for a few seconds and then announced, clearly, 'I've got to leave this room now!' and stood up. I was taken aback and for a while I simply sat watching him as he began wrapping himself back up in his various layers, and collecting his different belongings – his many bags, umbrella, scarf, gloves and hat. Finally I managed to get out a safely neutral reflection,

> *Sarah:* 'You feel the best way I can be a help to you at the moment is that we end the session early today?'
>
> *Eric:* 'Yes. Yes. I just want to go now.'
>
> *Sarah:* 'OK, Eric. I just want to check with you about what you want to do when you leave here.'
>
> *Eric:* 'Go home. Lie down. I'll be all right.'
>
> *Sarah:* 'That sounds soothing. I do want to be sure that you won't do something that might be risky or harmful to yourself.'
>
> *Eric:* 'No, no. I'm OK. Don't worry about that. Just... I'll be better once I'm home. I can't be here any more.'
>
> *Sarah:* 'OK.'

We walked into the hall and as we did do I could see, through the glass panels of the front door, that someone was coming up my garden path.

> *Sarah:* 'I'm so sorry, Eric, I think there seems to be some-one about to ring the doorbell. Maybe it's the post. Would you mind just taking a seat for a moment?'
>
> *Eric:* (Weakly) 'No, that's OK.'

I was expecting him to briefly return to the therapy room and take his seat there again, but as the doorbell did indeed ring, he simply sat down abruptly where he had been standing, which meant he was sitting on the bottom step of the stairs in my hall. I opened the door to a delivery man, feeling most disoriented by the many unexpected turns which the session had taken so far, but feeling as if I still had the process just about in my grasp. I would quickly sign for whatever package was being delivered and then be able to show Eric out.

> **Delivery man:** 'Can you take a delivery for next door – they're not answering.'
> **Sarah:** 'Umm. OK. But can it be quick, please.'
> **Delivery Man:** 'No problem. Quick as I can.'

Then, to my dismay, I saw the guy go to his van and begin to unload a series of large boxes, stacking them on the pavement as he did so, and I realized this was not going to be a quick process at all. I felt my containment of the session slipping away from under my fingertips. I stood at the door holding on to my impatience as he unloaded half a dozen sizable cardboard boxes, brought them over, in a number of trips to and from his van, scanned each one, and then got me to sign for each one.

At one point I looked behind me, ready to apologize to Eric for this delay and to see how he was. I was startled to see that a transformation had happened in the brief time he had taken a seat in my hall. From looking most jangled, distressed and exhausted, his manner had shifted; he now appeared relaxed, at ease, and rather as if he was enjoying himself. Indeed, he gave me a little smile and a wave as he looked over at me on the front doormat, looking, I imagine, rather flustered and put out.

The delivery man was in a mood to grumble and tried to tell me at some length about a woman he had delivered to earlier who had been rude to him. I tried several times, as tactfully as I could, to cut him short, or make it clear that I wasn't up for being a listening ear at this time. This did not succeed and the grumbling went on as he made his delivery. At one point I heard Eric give a short chuckle after I had attempted for the third time to get the delivery guy to stop talking and just finish the task. Finally, after about ten minutes of delay, when the delivery was over and the hall full of packages, and I felt thoroughly unprofessional and ruffled I turned again to Eric. He was now looking positively dreamy and peaceful on my stairs. He had leaned sideways so that he could rest his head against the wall of the hall, and was gazing off into the middle distance.

Later, my supervisor, with an amused smile, asked me what it was that had helped me keep going, and, despite all the pressures on the boundaries of this session, hold the therapeutic space for Eric. I thought for a while, and as I did so, many memories came tumbling back into my conscious awareness, about the times I had felt the benefit of others in this field being able to be flexible around boundaries, whilst still also being a container for the work. I remembered many trainers, therapists and supervisors over the years, who had all been willing to generously extend themselves, whilst staying grounded, and how deeply healing for me this had been. I learned from them all that therapy cannot be effective if it is governed by rigid rules, but that it is most effective when it feels human, responsive and relational, within certain boundaries that are not set in stone, but are grounded in something more organismic and adaptable.

I couldn't begin to tell my supervisor about all the times I had suddenly seen in my mind's eye, so I chose one particular instance:

> 'Well,' I said, 'I think in that regard, I'm simply walking along a trail that was blazed before me, a long time ago. I once did a term of group analysis with an old, semi-retired analyst who had actually been trained by and worked with Winnicott. In one group I had been talking about my horrible work pressures, and as I left, he had put his hand on my shoulder and gave it a slight squeeze as he said goodbye. It made a big impression on the young me – I was only in my late twenties and had all sorts of stiff ideas about how analysts should never touch patients. It had felt kind, but unfamiliar too. It was a time in my life when I wasn't getting

many kind shoulder squeezes. At the next group, I asked him about it: he hadn't squeezed anyone else's shoulder – why mine? I had asked him, in a slightly ungrateful, stroppy tone, it has to be said. With a grandfatherly smile, he simply said 'I judged you to be needing a little bit of extra support just then'.

I felt tears prick my eyes as I retold this to my supervisor, and felt again both the truth of that experienced analyst's observation, and his kindly willingness to stick his neck out (and, more literally, his hand) in order to offer a stressed, confused, young woman the warmth and encouragement she had been lacking just then.

Sarah: *'OK, Eric. The coast's clear at last.'*

He stirred from what seemed a state of reverie and got up. He seemed in a much better state after his little sojourn in the hall, and said goodbye in his usual courteous way. I wondered after he had gone and I was writing my notes, about how happy and contented he had seemed as he had waited, in contrast to how uncomfortable and harried I had been feeling. Perhaps, I mused there had been something very 'right' for Eric in the 'wrongness' of having to wait in my hall. Perhaps what had happened was that I had committed Jung's paradoxical *felix culpa or blessed sin*.[10]

Seen through one lens, the fact that I had allowed a client to sit in my hallway while a delivery man brought box after box into my hall meant I had failed to maintain a professional, boundaried space for the client. But seen through another lens, I had given the client an important opportunity to re-work something that was crucial to his therapy because I had managed not to be like the mother of his youth in three respects:

- I had managed not to blame and shame him for a bit of carelessness.

- I had respected his autonomy and not prevented him from leaving the session early.

- And, with fate's helpful intervention, I had had to tolerate the irritating muddle and imperfection of the sort of day-to-day stuff that happens in a family home, in front of Eric, while he simply spent time in that home and things happened around him that he had no responsibility for.

Because of all this, Eric had been able to have a visceral experience of revisiting an old territory – family life - and find something new in it.

An attacking, destructive energy had certainly burst, painfully and disorientatingly, into the session early on: through Eric's unconscious attack on my son's book, through my embodied urge to re-enact the Negative-Mother reaction of shaming and blaming the 'wrong doer', and with Eric's reconnection to how hateful and terrifying he had sometimes experienced his mother when he was little. But by hanging onto the possibility that whatever was constellating between us had potential meaning and value, I had managed to help us both digest and make meaning of some toxic sensations that Eric normally found so dreadful and confusing, in himself and others, and so had often been unable to integrate within himself. Just as he had once, naturally, struggled with being forced to ingest a wax crayon alongside the annihilating aggression from his mother with which it had been presented.

Perhaps in that difficult, muddly session, he and I had been involved in untangling some of the '*dark briars*' that had been binding Eric's '*joys and desires*' for so long, and which had turned his garden of love into a gloomy place of forbidding priests and tombstones. For any of us to feel that the garden of love can truly be trusted, it has to be a place where it is clear that shadowy experiences such as rage, disgust and conflict also have their place. It is not a space where joy and desire must be split off and kept separate from aggression and hatred. The every day garden of love is one where love is non-showy, not inflated or aiming for perfection, but instead it is a place where there is a love on offer that can be deeply relied upon to accept every single human emotion, and make a place to feel and think about them all. It was my own deeply embodied experiences of having been received and held in such a kind of reliable, everyday love – particularly in my own therapy, and during the training at Re-Vision - that meant I could hold out the hope to Eric that there might exist such a place of deep compassion for him, too: a garden he also could enter, in which he could find a healing acceptance of shadowy feelings, as well as joyful ones, which would provide balm for his anguish.

In the very next session Eric named what this new experience of allowing an expression of and more consciously integrating some destructive anger in the session had been like.

> **Eric:** *'It was nice, afterwards. Quite good fun actually, to just sit in your hall. There was nothing for me to do, no pressure. I mean, you weren't going to ask me anything, you were just having to deal with that guy. It was funny. Nice. I liked just sitting there, watching you sort the delivery out. I could just be in the background and watch.'*

We wondered together if what Eric had experienced in the hall had been the sort of experience he had longed to have more of as a boy – more forgiveness for the small slips and mishaps of everyday, and more chances just to 'be' in a caregiver's presence, trusting that they can handle mishaps and outbursts, and still make sure things in the home go more or less smoothly, despite life's ups and downs (including unpredictable and inconvenient deliveries), able to believe that 'good enough' will have to do.

After this messy and unsettling session, there was a most remarkable and quite rapid change in much of Eric's life. His drinking dwindled away so that within a few months he was hardly drinking at all. Many of his eccentric behaviours also lessened, and although he sometimes still brought me little objects of beauty he had found on walks, they were of the more usual kind you might pick up and show a friend, such as a feather, stone, or shell. He joined a local art appreciation group and also began to study Italian at an adult education centre. In both his classes he met a few like-minded people with whom he began to socialize on a regular basis. About three months after 'the hall way session' (as I tended to think of it), he announced excitedly at the start of a session that he had been asked out on 'a real date' by one of the women in his

Italian class, and that they were planning to go to an art exhibition and then for a coffee.

A few months after this, Eric and I drew his therapy to a close, at his choosing. He had been coming for just over three years. By then he felt more hopeful about finding a relationship, he was not drinking, was much less depressed and anxious, more able to manage his sensitive stomach, and was feeling that he had things to offer and projects he wanted to see through in the future.

He was also more able to remember and think about his early childhood and the impact that some of his parents' behaviour had had on him without feeling overwhelmed by inarticulate-able despair, fury and grief. A few weeks before we ended our therapy, he travelled North to visit his parents in the old family home. They were both now very elderly and frail. Eric talked a little with them about his childhood experiences, and told me that although they did not say so in so many words, he came away feeling that they had heard what he had to say and wanted to convey some regret for the times they had been harsh with him; he had felt sure they were pleased to see him and they actually told him they were very glad he had made the effort to visit.

It seemed fitting that the last thing Eric brought me, as a goodbye gift on the day we had our least session, was a poem. It was 'Sometimes a Wild God' by Tom Hirons. The last stanza reads:

> Sometimes a wild god comes to the table
> He is awkward and does not know the ways
> Of porcelaine, of fork and mustard and silver
> His voice makes vinegar from wine
> And brings the dead to life.[11]

1 Carl Gustav Jung, *Two Essays on Analytical Psychology* (New York: Dodd, Mead & Co. 1928), p. 3.

2 William Plotkin, *Soulcraft: Crossing into the Mysteries of Nature and Psyche* (Novato, CA: New World Library, 2003), p. 250.

3 James Hillman, *The Essential James Hillman: A Blue Fire*, ed. Thomas Moore (London: Routledge, 1990), pp. 114 – 121.

4 John Ryan Haule, *The Love Cure: Therapy Erotic and Sexual* (Woodstock, CT: Spring Publications, 1996), p. 53.

5 Thomas Stearns Eliot, *Four Quartets: The Dry Salvages* (London: Faber & Faber Ltd., 1944), p. 28.

6 William Wordsworth, 'Intimations of Immortality from Recollections of Early Childhood', in *The Penguin Book of English Romantic Verse*, ed. D. Wright (London: Penguin Books, 1968), p. 139. Poem first published in 1888.

7 William Blake, *Songs of Innocence and Experience* (Oxford: Oxford University Press, 1970), p. 150 (Plate 44). Poem first published in 1789.

8 Michael Balint, *The Basic Fault* (London: Tavistock Publications Ltd., 1968), p. 66.

9 Martin Buber, *I and Thou*, trans. Walter Kaufman (New York: Touchstone, 1996).

10 Carl Gustav Jung, *C G Jung. Letters. Vol 2, 1951 -1961*, ed. Gerhard Adler (Hove: Routledge, 1976), p. 202.

11 Tom Hirons, *Sometimes a Wild God* (London: Hedgespoken Press, 2015), p. 28. Used with the author's permission.

Chapter 5

Soul and Soulmaking

Chris Robertson

> Words are delicious, but cannot say much. They often lose
> the water of meaning before it is delivered. But they can
> be stirred to form descriptions of the breath, glances, ges-
> tures, and pulses between lives. Perhaps writing is finding
> a scrape in the skin of knowing, where the sting and dirt
> and blood of the day is let out, and music is let in.
> —Bateson[1]

The Bateson quote above offers the possibility of moist dialogue
in which the water of meaning and the music of the soul get ex-
changed. If Psyche, as soul, originally meant the breath of life, then
it is through the exchange of that breath with spoken words, half
utterances, sighs, howls, pitiful moans, rueful mumbles, raging
yells and breathy silences that make up the often intense and intimate coalescence within therapy.

What is speaking through that space between the therapeutic
couple as they share that same air? How to translate the vernacular
nature of the craft into the written word? While ensouled speech
imaginatively evokes the feeling and connects the therapy partners, abstract language robs the soul of its mythic richness. Writing about soul inevitably means a loss of the water of meaning and
perhaps we can learn from the poets how to sound into those gaps,
rather than follow diagnosticians.

The guide for writing case studies at Re-Vision begins:

> A case study is firstly a challenge to tell one of Psyche's
> stories. A story of healing; a story which reveals some-
> thing of Psyche herself and so becomes a healing story.
> Through the medium of the case something about the
> therapeutic art is being remembered and revealed, but

not explained. Through the writing of a case, authors reveal something of their craft and at the same time are led to recognise Psyche's hand at work. Through witnessing this therapeutic adventure, the reader is led to see something of themselves mirrored back and something not of themselves. So we are led both into ourselves and beyond ourselves.

The above guide reflects Hillman's exploration of what the soul wants and what it shuns.[2] He picks out literalism as the chief culprit of psychological literature. What soul wants is a *guiding fiction* – a story within which the client recognizes his or her defeats, rejections and betrayals. Successful therapy, he suggests, is '... a revisioning of the story into a more intelligent, imaginative plot, which also means the sense of mythos in all parts of the story'.[3] The 'mythos' is what connects the plot with the sacred.

My own guiding fiction began in the 1980's by researching the etymology of therapy in a very old dictionary. What I remember reading was about the *Therapae*, the Greek maidens who served in the temples of Asclepius to prepare the supplicants for a sacred dream. There needed to be an atmosphere of receptive waiting in the preparation for these dreams, which reflects the attentive receptivity of therapeutic awareness. Years later it seemed that the *Therapae* did not exist. Searching in dictionaries only offered the *Therapeutae*, who were an ancient order of mystical ascetics and healers – similar but not specifically addressing dreams. Yet the memory of the original research was striking and the notion of a very old dictionary suggests a dream. So now the memory has become a fiction. Whether the memory was a dream or not, it became a guiding fiction for how I imagined a therapy that was soulful.

This chapter will venture into the mythopoetic landscape of soul with the hope of finding, as Nora Bateson describes it, a 'scrape in the skin of knowing, where the sting and the dirt and the blood of the day is let out'. By shifting our perception, our consciousness no longer proceeds out from the eyes in my head but occupies the space in-between; that relational space within which the therapeutic couple interact; that space that holds us; that feminine vessel that incubates a fertile imagination and draws a silver presence towards us.

Here is an excerpt from such a landscape:

> *I sit opposite my client Andrew. We have sat here before; like two persons come to invoke a presence or await a higher authority. We wait for that wind to blow through us. He sighs more in anticipation than resignation as the words find their way to his speech. I feel a slight tightening of my muscles, my animal senses reaching out for what may be emerging between us. It is as if we are on a tracking session together, smelling the wind and attempting to read the half-hidden signs.*[4]

In this animate landscape, the wind seems to give rise to the words, which find their own way to be spoken. There is anticipation. We are sensing the phenomena along with the characters. Similarly Jill Hayes writes,

> When soul enters the room the air thickens. It is as if the air becomes rich with meaning. Not a meaning we can grasp with our intellect or our rationality. But a full-bodied meaning that temporarily suspends us in time. The speaking of someone's truth has a resonance like a church bell, which shakes us into a spell of noticing what we often miss about each other.[5]

With the entry of soul, meaning thickens, like a plot thickening. Hayes suggests that we can feel it in the air. It's a presence that heightens our senses. It is not a concept confined to linguistic analysis. The meaning is not in the words; it is felt in the presence. Poets have led the way and novelists follow in their characterization of soulful moments. Yet stories that touch the soul are common in the consulting room. What happened to this presence?

The notion of 'soul' used to be the prerogative of religious discourse and was shunned by psychology in its desire for scientific objectivity and recognition. The academic requirement for explanations robbed 'soul' of its inherent meaning and vitality. The re-claiming of soul into psychological discourse was begun by Jung in his early notions of Anima and developed as essential to the process of individuation. Drawing on indigenous lore, Jung diag-nosed the predicament of modern cultures as the 'loss of soul' and the analyst's task was, like the medicine men, to help its retrieval through finding meaning in life.[6] He recounts an interview with a woman patient whose complaint was that she had lost her heart. When the psychiatrist asked her to put her hand on her chest to feel her heart beating, she replied, 'That is not my real heart.'[7]

Whereas the soul defies conceptual definition, this short anec-dote supports soulful imaginings about what had happened to this woman's heart. Had she lost it in love? Was she in deep grief? Had she sold her soul in a false bargain? Had one she trusted betrayed her? Or had the vital juices of her life dried up, leaving her bereft of connection and devoid of vitality? Such fantasies do not abstract into objectified medical terms but draw on poetic metaphors that are akin to the speech of the soul. As described in Chapter 1, 'Roots and Seeds', the heart has been central to the feelings of soul, both the anguish of abandonment and the yearnings for connection.

Hillman suggest that soul:[8]

- Refers to the deepening of events into experiences.

- Makes things significant through its special relation with death.

- Is experienced through our imaginative nature.

The speech of the soul entails these three movements. Within therapeutic dialogue the deepening of events into experience helps therapist and client recognize how the client has organized events in their life into a story that gave meaning. Such meanings are mutable, and if colonized by the ego, can become rehearsed and arid. Awakenings are defended against by the ego, which prefers its known continuum. As Bion wrote of his group analytic practice, the impulse for new experience is in conflict with de-fences against the anxiety they produce.[9] The experiences of dis-appointment and disillusionment are simultaneously shunned (by the ego) yet are potentially transformative. It takes something like a death, a dying into new life, to allow defences to release into a new vitality.

When such charged moments happen in therapy, it is our imaginative natures that catalyze the surrender of ego and open the door to soul. Such a moment is exemplified in the first part of Morgan Farley's poem:

> I know there is another way to live.
> When I find it, the angels
> will cry out in rapture,
> each cell of my body
> will be a rose, a star.
> If something seized my life tonight,
> if a sudden wind swept through me,
> changing everything,
> I would not resist.
> I am ready for whatever comes.[10]

This chapter attempts to speak to soul in fresh ways and listen with new ears. It explores three of the many dimensions of soul making that are particularly vital to the Re-Vision approach.

1   The shift from ego stories, the talking about the client's life, that often takes up therapy space, to a dropping down into a symbolic process of engaged participation – this is the deepening of events into experience of which Hillman wrote. This is expanded below in the section below, **Soul Talk**.

2   Soulmaking is intimately connected with wounding and healing. As Hillman suggests, 'Building the psychic vessel of containment, which is another way of speaking of soul-making, seems to require bleeding and leaking as its precondition'.[11] This wounding includes suicidal ideation and the soul's intimate connection with death and the underworld. This is expanded under the title **The Underworld of Soulmaking**.

3   The heart's longing, it's yearning for re-connecting from
    what we have been separated is the work of soulmaking.
    'This yearning is suffering and is a sign of soul sickness
    and also of movement. Eros gives psyche this yearning'.[12]
    We could call this transference but it is not something
    transferred simply from frustrated infant needs. This is
    expanded under the section **On Being Love Sick**.

Soul Talk

The difference between ego and psyche isn't only theoretical; it's in how you tell a story. It's in getting the sub-
jectivity out of it, so the story, the image takes over.[13]

Soul is not mine. I do not own a soul. Contrary to the emphasis
on individuality and personal salvation so dominant in Western
cultures, the emphasis here is on soul having a collective character
– the *anima mundi* or ensouled world. Soul is not only a human
entitlement; it is the animating principle in our world. It is recognition that the world is sensing us as we are sensing it. We live in
a reciprocal world in which we are not the privileged spectator but
a potentially engaged participant.

Walking or just being in a natural environment can open a portal for our attention to switch out of the narrow focus of ego consciousness. We can suddenly become aware of being watched, of
being in that reciprocal relationship of which we are not in control. It is not simply 'me' walking up the hill but the hill inviting
me into a mutual engagement. An indigenous hunter and their
prey are in a mutual dance. It is not a one-way pursuit. The hunter
allows a defocused attention that is not expecting anything. This
ecological perception of participatory engagement is a great model
for a paradigm shift in therapeutic thinking and practice. We are
not stalking the client anymore than they us. We are in a dynamic
presence that draws us into relationship.

Our most immediate experience of things is necessarily
an experience of reciprocal encounter – of tension, communication, and commingling. From within the depths of

this encounter, we know the thing or phenomenon only as our interlocutor – as a dynamic presence that confronts us and draws us into relation.[14]

I have previously written about a client, called 'Jason', who had a deep resonance with the magic of the horses.[15] He felt this resonance was what kept his soul alive in a desecrated world that he had inhabited as a sensitive child. Telling stories about his relation to horses brought their magic into the room. They offered an alternative to the domestication to which he felt he had to submit. In this deeper sense he had felt himself a victim to external forces – powers over which he had no apparent say – and without the 'horsepower', he might have succumbed to despair. Through the telling of these stories he began to retell his own story. We moved from stories about his past to imaginative stories co-created between us that reflected his present dilemma.

Psychotherapy stories take us through a history of relations; the varied paths that cross and intersect through the client's life and somehow interweave with that of the therapist. Often the client's story appears like a dream – one that is dreaming them. The outer event materializes in the therapy room. Continuing the story with Andrew (above):

> He brings a dream: a visitation during the night that wants a second appearance. He is on a cliff with his partner looking out to the sea. Immediately I am there with them noticing together with him a wave slowly building in the far distance. From previous dreams he recognizes that this is potential tsunami. He points it out to his partner and as we watch, it is drawing the ocean up into itself. He tells her that they must get back from the cliff's edge – he knows the power of this elemental force. But she does not respond. Like a prey caught in a hypnotic trance, she is immoveable, ignoring his increasingly desperate pleas.
>
> In a terrifying engulfment the huge wave breaks across the cliff and as the spray clears, she has gone. The slight imprint of her feet left is still on the grass. After a shocked silence, Andrew rushes to the cliff edge. Much to his surprise

*he sees her on the beach below and as he watches, he can
see that she is moving. She is alive!*

*Back in the dry of the consulting room, we both tremble
at the retelling of this visitation. Although the dream visitor
has gone, she, like the partner, has left her imprint. There is
the tang of salt in the air and a feeling of bewilderment. We
might think that the psyche is inside of us or that dreams
happen inside a person's head, but clearly we were inside
this dream.*

We could say that the aim of soulmaking is to be inside the
dream – to enter imaginatively into the experience. It helps me
when listening to a client's life story to imagine that they are
telling me a dream. This allows me to imagine that the characters
of whom the client is speaking are visitors in his/her dream. And
in a way they are. It is not random whom the client chooses to
speak about. They are creating a fiction about themselves to engage me. While it is a shade provocative to say, as Robert Avens
does, that *Imagination is Reality*, the imaginative reworking of the
client's story is central to psychotherapy practice.[16] The consulting
room becomes an imaginal space within which new possibilities
reveal themselves.

Hillman writes:

> Outside and inside, life and soul, appear as parallels in
> "case history" and "soul history." A case history is a biog-
> raphy of historical events in which one took part: family,
> school, work, illnesses, war, love. The soul history often
> neglects entirely some or many of these events, and
> spontaneously invents fictions and "inscapes" without
> major outer correlations. The biography of the soul con-
> cerns experience.[17]

As inside/outside becomes a false dichotomy, the notion that
culture has its place within the confines of the consulting room is
finally recognized. It is not just the family, let alone just 'mother',
that is the source of our values, our ego expectations of life and
how we attempt to get our needs met. Just as Winnicott said,

'There is no such thing as a baby', we can say that there is no such thing as an individual.[18] Trailing behind the client like a ghostly trail is the miniculture network of inter-relations, hidden rules, sweet and traumatic encounters, ancestral hauntings and emergent paths to new potentials that intermingle to make his/her story enfolded within the larger cultural story.

Ingold writes that we live in a storied world in which we know people through knowing their story. 'We identify things in the world through the paths they make through the unfolding field of relations - how they intertwine through getting into each others stories'.[19]

Mostly clients have simplified their story and if the therapist colludes with a reduction into a family narrative or DSM type categories then the complexity with its wonderful diversity, richness and confusion gets lost. Psychotherapy training risks inducting students into maps and models as the means to understand and control the uncertainty of the therapeutic relationship. We know from Korzybski that the map is not the territory but when anxious, it is easy to forget and reach for the comfort blanket of a reassuring known.

How to bear the complexity? Not so much a comfort blanket but a means of self-soothing, of managing the tension of not-knowing, is essential. Students in the training at Re-Vision learn early that their sense of confusion has value in itself. They learn to refrain from attempts to explain and sort it out. Richness of meaning and ambiguity go together. So staying with the focus of discomfort, the dis-ease is a central task to open what has previously been closed off, defended against – assuming that there is sufficient containment to hold this uncertainty. This is the practice of *negative capability* (explored further in Chapter 9, 'Knowing of a Third Kind') that requires both a letting go of goal seeking and a letting go to the seeming chaotic complexity.

The dynamic field of the therapeutic couple has a permeable membrane that filters what can be thought. It filters out what could be threatening either in the sense of being dangerous to previous trauma that could be triggered or dangerous in the potency that certain potentialities carry. These may be intolerable to old identifications formed out of bonds of loyalty or unconscious promises. At such rich thresholds in therapy, where the old skin is no longer adequate, how can a transformation be allowed? What allows a caterpillar to transform into a butterfly? The therapist's presence within the permeable bubble offers holding and catalyzes new kinds of stories that can include what was previously excluded or misunderstood. Working through the painful emotions towards an acceptance of losses, wounds and hateful enactments can shift the underlying stream of the story from ego-familiar to a creative confusion.

Just as the craft of psychotherapy would be better described as a listening cure, the ensouling process has more to do with listening and being heard than of talking. The craft entails listening for that change of tone (a discordant harmony), the unfinished sentence, the pregnant pause, what is unsaid but felt as emergent. The quality of trust that you will be heard can catalyze the courage to risk speaking these 'missing' possibilities. Re-Vision students have both their own therapy and the training group as models for this craft. The training group offers a heightened awareness of how these soulful spaces can be perceived – a listening through to those excluded margins – and called forth from the underground stream of relationship.

Working with a training group, I notice a feeling of something missing from the field between us. My loose intention was to move into some practical work but this feeling draws my attention. It is always difficult to attend to what is missing; it is a resonance with something unspoken or not attended to. I name this and one member who has not previously contributed begins to speak. She feels rather out of the group, on the margins. Other participants encourage her to join in and fail to grasp that their well-meaning invitation is part of the problem as it feels like an implicit rule that says people need to be clear about their participation. As we stay with the difficulties, moving from thoughts to a sensing of what is present, other members begin to own their discomfort with her ambivalence and this creates the space to recognise how she carries shadow ambivalences for this "open, accepting group".[20]

The point is that the person marginalized in the group will often feel excluded by implicit group norms. Here within this 'open, accepting group', she was the deviant who held the shadow of ambivalence. Her silence is what spoke in the sense of a present absence or an absence that made itself present through her silence. This brings us to the strange thing about soul – that it is often in that sense of something missing that we can feel its presence.

This is the field of soul talk that includes pregnant silence. This is the deepening into experience where words regain their felt meaning; where the beautiful, painful shedding of ego skins that catch unbearable cultural wounds can be spoken and heard.

The Underworld of Soulmaking

The dread and resistance which every natural human being experiences when it comes to delving too deeply into him or herself is, at bottom, the fear of the journey to Hades.[21]

The quote from Jung describes his own experience in entering that dark time in his life. A descent into the depth involves passing through this dread, being willing to enter into the dark unseen, that which is below the surface. Such descents happen at formative thresholds when a person, group or collective have to reach deep within themselves to find the resources to meet an ensuing crisis. The treasures that Jung brought back are revealed in his extraordinary Red Book.[22]

This reaching deep within requires a sacrifice of conscious knowing and control. The underworld appears when we 'go under'. The relinquishing of ego consciousness may not happen easily, for the loss of control feels like dying. When the therapist as well as the client is affected by this fear, the underworld can be shunned while the therapy focuses on sorting out the dayworld problems and supporting the client to make more of their life. The therapist has to develop a 'perverse sensibility' to the pull of the underworld – a sort of undertow that is sensed in the relational field. Why perverse? Because the fantasies that allow entry into this underworld are not the healthy sunshine ones. It is what lies in the shadow of the controlling ego's earthly plans for success. It lies in the complexes that keep a client sabotaging their career or romantic opportunities or those paranoid fantasies that they have infected their partner with, like some toxic illness.

These notions of soulmaking are in contrast to some humanistic concerns with seeing the best in the client that leave little place for the dark shadow. As Hillman points out, 'To humanize means not just loving and forgiving; it means as well torturing and vengeance and every cravenness that history will not let us forgive'.[23] Hillman insists that soulmaking is not simply making better human connections. He states that, 'Feeling that is a merely human function loses its power to reflect the psyche beyond the human to the unknowns of the soul'.[24] Hillman, drawing on Jung, says that guides to the land of the dead reveal the primacy of the psyche.[25] He claims that, 'It is in the light of the psyche that we must read all underworld descriptions. Being in the underworld means psychic being, being psychological, where soul comes first'.[26]

The descent into the underworld is not a conceptual understanding. It shatters the ego ideal and opens the door to soul. It is an imaginal journey through terror, torture, tragedy and mystery graphically described in such myths as Persephone being carried down (raped) by Hades, Orpheus's doomed attempt to retrieve his beloved Eurydice, and Inanna, the Sumerian Goddess, being stripped of all her regalia and power to be hung on a meat hook. Through enduring psychic pains and grieving terrible losses, we become more permeable and paradoxically potent. The descent often takes the form of a melancholic hopelessness, so difficult for a therapist to stay with without resorting to rescue.

The troubles that we may suffer in the course of living are not mistakes to be transcended on the way to a more spiritual path. The classic question asked of patients is, 'What is wrong with you', which implies a pathological framework and corrective treatment. The key point in Hillman's revisioning of psychopathology is that suffering is not only something not to be voided by being drugged out of consciousness, but is intrinsic to a soulful life. Hillman says:

> Our attempt to envision pathologizing psychologically is
> to find a place for it, a way of accepting it, in general and
> as a whole. We want to know what it might be saying
> about the soul and what the soul might be saying by
> means of it.[27]

Giving a place to our troubles may be counter-cultural in our overly safe, pain avoidant culture. Finding such a place that does not deny the pain and suffering but provides a deeper framework, in which the wounding has potential meaning, is the work of soul-making. In Aeschylus's play of the trial of Orestes for the killing of his mother (matricide), Athena has to deal with the Furies' reaction to her not guilty judgement. She understands that these primal instinctual forces must not remain outcast – they need their own place of honour, which she grants them. Similarly for a soulful approach to psychotherapy, we need to support the client in giving a place to these painful wounds which otherwise would be outcast into the shadow. This simple and neutral phrase, 'to give a place' to the troubles one has suffered has soothed many a primitive fury by honouring their voice rather than denying or denigrating them. By giving a place we are not lauding suffering or being grateful to the perpetrators of our wounding. We are simply acknowledging that wounding is intrinsic to life and potentially meaningful.

Not all suffering is soulmaking. Some internalized violence seems beyond repair, especially where the client has suffered the trauma of soul murder. This term was first used by Shengold to describe the devastating consequences of childhood abuse that systematically destroy the creative playful capacities of a child.[28] While the soul cannot be literally murdered, the soulmaking process can be deadened, leaving the person desolated (literally de-souled). Kalsched's work on *Defences of the Self* helps understand how daimonic forces of the Self 'rescue' the abused traumatized person but at the cost of their being imprisoned within the self-care system that refuses to allow any creative movement that would make them vulnerable to further attack.[29] Kalsched quotes Simone Weil as saying, 'The false god turns suffering into violence; the true god turns violence into suffering'.[30]

There is a thin line between what Kalsched terms *Defences of the Self* and the internalized violence, the self-hatred that tries to blot out suffering. This can lead to terrible depression and sometimes suicide. Rosen started his study of depression with research on those who had survived suicide attempts.[31] Many reported that, through this descent into what Rosen calls *egocide*, a symbolic death, a miraculous transformation happened. Important though this is in recognizing descent as necessary for transformation through death of the false self, it is difficult not to wonder if his research was biased by not being able to interview those whose suicide had been 'successful'.

Depression is the shadow side of our manic culture, speeding onto the next things without any digestion of the present but driven on by the industry of distraction and 'hope for the wrong thing', as T. S. Elliot called it. Hillman writes, 'Through depression we enter depths and in depths find soul. It moistens the dry soul, and dries the wet. It brings refuge, limitations, focus, gravity, weight and humble powerlessness. It reminds us of death. The true revolution begins in the individual who can be true to his own depression'.[32]

Thomas Moore, author of *Care of the Soul* and Re-Vision's patron, suggests that our society's fixation on light means that in compensation we will suffer depression more strongly. He is not wrong. The NHS prescribes approximately sixty-five million antidepressants each year and it is growing. Clearly this is as much a cultural symptom as it is individual, even if it is as individuals that we suffer it. For those courageous enough to bring their depression to therapy, they carry a cultural shadow with them, which they may take personally. It is vital for the therapist to recognize this collective dimension to the personal symptoms. Being true to his/her own depression also means not taking on what does not belong, not becoming a scapegoat for a cultural pathology.

The smaller version of this is a family pathology in which the parents load their children with their own unfulfilled expectations. Taken personally, the inevitable disappointments feel like letting down the family. Somewhat paradoxically this letting down is the necessary journey towards individuation. Not surprisingly this sense of *let down* can often appear in the relational field as the client or therapist not feeling good enough. If these symptoms are not taken as 'wrong' and in need of correction, they can drop the therapeutic encounter into a deeper level of work.

These downward movements, a natural part of life, can become charged within the therapeutic or training relationship where idealized hopes and unrealistic investments are an inevitable part of the process. Therapy is inherently frustrating as it evokes the hopes for what has been neglected. Similarly, training relationships require the confronting of limitations and the appreciation of the value of boundaries. Rather than a narcissistic endeavour to please, facing into the disappointment and disillusionment as soul work, as a move downwards into our depths, can be satisfyingly real.

Within Re-Vision's training, this downward movement is highlighted through listening and valuing students' own stories of wounding and suffering. The wheel below outlines different phases of descent.

The first phase, pre-ego depression, is characterized as 'sulking' – an angry turning away. The threshold activates separation and release from family bonds, but relative failures and a lack of grieving for ideal relationships that have not been available lead to melancholic depression. The second threshold offers another chance for mourning losses and transforming bitterness. The falling into Hades, surrender as opposed to resignation, is vital here for the transformation and willingness to re-engage with the troubles of family life. As the wheel implies, this is an ongoing cycle, not a once and for all breakthrough.

John Keats, from whom Hillman borrowed the notion of soul-making, thought that the making of soul required the heart to endure the sufferings of life. He describes the heart as a breast from which the mind may draw an identity, like milk from a 'teat' or breast. He wrote in his letter to his sister and brother, 'Do you not see how necessary a World of Pains and troubles is to school an Intelligence and make it a soul! A Place where the heart must feel and suffer in a thousand diverse ways!'[33]

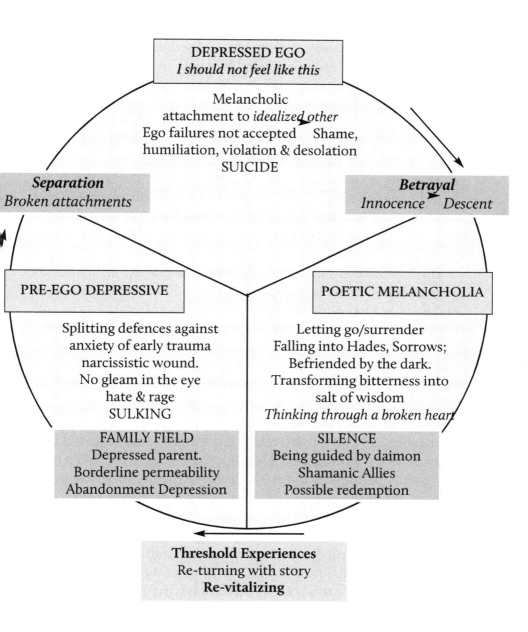

Figure 5.1. The Re-Vision Depression Wheel.

Hillman suggests that knowing our wounds is a precondition for soulmaking. Being altogether won't work as an initial condition. This way is the way of becoming vulnerable, becoming open, and learning how to bear our troubles without denial.

The heroic refusal to go down, to fight on, and not to acknowledge wounding, creates its own suffering. It is the suffering I inflict on myself in my refusal to learn, to soften and acknowledge vulnerability. This often leads to repeated cycles (repetition compulsion) – cycles that maintain my neurosis and have the pay-off of avoiding the existential threshold in the wound. This is the point when I *could* choose to attend to the wounds of my childhood (which I could not have as a child) but now fail to by continuing a victim story of my past that refuses the responsibility of becoming the author of my story.

This refusal can take a circular form – a shifting avoidance of the existential challenge of facing into shadow. A manic defence is vigilant against any relaxation that might soften the skin and allow a fall – a fall into something shameful, dark and unknown. In contrast the depressive defence claims a fragile victimhood of passive entitlement without any requirement for responsibility. Both manic and depressive operate as psychic prisons. But as Kafka recognized, such prison bars are wide enough to allow a prisoner out if they so choose.[34]

The angst in even considering that freedom can make it a terrifying taboo. Somewhat like Kalsched's defences of the self, a border guard operates to question your permit. It involves some trespass, breaking a boundary, betraying a promise, an unconscious promise to a parent that has held the child in thrall to some implicit expectation.[35] On the wheel above, it operates at the second threshold, marked as Betrayal. Although there can be personal slights that we may feel as let downs of what we expect, betrayal signifies dropping into a crevice, a gulf of terrifying depth. Betrayal marks the end of naivety and an awakening into the complexity of soulmaking. In order to learn being true to our own path, it is inevitable that we will betray loyalty to others to whom we have been bound. This is the pain that accompanies another birthing.

For a therapist not to become caught up in a collusive repertoire of helpful strategies, they have to be willing to risk vitriolic transference, as if they are the betrayer that persecutes the client. What is at stake? A false loyalty to the defences of the ego that do not want to surrender to that dark side of soul. This is the threshold that Hillman describes as going from Anima-vessel towards humility.[36] Releasing oneself from the prison of feeling sorry for self and bearing the pain of life's wounding. Not heroically but through giving up the hope for escape, for rescue, for some good parent to come.

This good parent can constellate in the therapist as a helper or rescuer. This Florence Nightingale complex can be a dangerous force – a corruption of love by the illusion of superior knowing what is needed; as Adolph Guggenbuhl-Craig pointed out, a split in the healing archetype gives all the power to the therapist and leaves the client dependent.[37] Therapists may require an inoculation with disillusionment in order to recognize the psychological materialism at work in the attempt to take away pain and remove suffering. Rescuing the client from their distress makes for a quiet time for both parties but is not good music for a soul dance.

After working on this process in the training, a student wrote:

> I remember where I have come from
> Dream fragments
> Cold terror
> Heated frenzy
> Rage
> Contempt
> DISS-memberment
> And then 'the blade so sharp it cuts together'

On Being Love Sick

We could make a case for seeing most clients' issues as suffering from love sickness in one form or another, since the need for love is so basic. It is this need for love and love as an emotion on which we now focus our attention while recognising that the dimensions of love are vast and various.[38]

This third section explores the heart's longing, its yearning for re-connecting from what we have been separated as the work of soulmaking. The tragic quality of suffering in love sickness drops us into a romantic field that poets have been ploughing for eons. This archetype takes form in disappointing love relations, movies and novels of heartbreak. One of the moist poignant love stories involving betrayal, the pining of unrequited love and also the terrible beauty and exquisite sensibility evoked by complete surrender to the beloved, is that of Yusuf and Zulaikha.[39] Theirs was a story of differing levels of adoration – the meeting of the fire of sexual Eros with pure divine love. There is some overlap with the story of Eros and Psyche in that once Psyche is freed from her unconscious unseeing relation with Eros by the jealousy of her sisters, she is set on her own journey of individuation through the torments of her heart to be reunited with Eros.

Soulmaking is explored in Psyche's tasks or labours, through which she gives birth to her true feminine self. I have previously written a detailed commentary on Psyche's labours as she moves from innocent girl to wounded woman in relation to a developing therapeutic relationship.[40] Psyche's journey through her different trials can, Hillman suggests, be read as initiatory.[41]

> The ordeals of Psyche and Eros are initiatory; they are symbolic of the psychic and erotic ordeals to which we are put. This gives us a wholly different view, not only of transference and analytical suffering, but also of the ground of neurosis in our time. Neurosis becomes an initiation, analysis the ritual, and our developmental process in Psyche and Eros, leading to their union, becomes the mystery.

While Psyche and Eros are tormented by their separation, the work done in that separating process allows a reunion at a deeper level – a movement from fused unity to a differentiated union. Hillman, in a deeply meditative text, reviews how different levels of the heart combine together to imagine love and allow love to imagine.[42] He distinguishes three levels of the heart; mythical, physical and imaginal. The third level, the soul of the heart, is the place of intimacy, mystery and desire for the divine where the appreciation of beauty brings out the aesthetic nature of soul. In a similar way, we could imagine three levels of erotic encounter that bear close resemblance to Psyche's challenges.

- The first involves an unconscious physiological attraction that we could characterize as pre-oedipal, as in the infant's need for the mother and the mother's need to bond with her infant.

- The second requires a more interactive engagement and a probable testing out of boundaries by the client, which the therapist needs to frustrate (the abstinence rule) in order to prevent the imaginal feeling getting literalized.

- The third is the place of potential mutuality, often missing within psychoanalytic texts, within which a sacred space of imaginal love can constellate.

Before we can allow love to imagine in psychotherapy, we have to work with the familiar issue of loss of control. The dangers of acting out of erotic countertransference are real and the principle of abstinence that guards the trust given to a psychotherapist by their clients is vital. The shadow side of this rule is the tendency to push the erotic feelings back onto the client and to deny that the therapist has reciprocal feelings. Schaverien describes many of the classic dilemmas in *Desire and the Female Therapist*.[43] The problem is that when these dilemmas become taboos, defensive practice and secrecy become a norm that inflates the shadow. The psychotherapeutic profession surrounds itself with boundaries and rules to guard against Eros's mad compulsion. Like Odysseus, we are told to strap ourselves to the mast when sailing into the waters where sirens dwell.

While much of the debate in psychoanalytic circles revolves round the dilemmas of how much disclosure of their erotic fantasies therapists should offer, and whether the erotic transference is Oedipal or pre-oedipal, the focus here is on the staying with the trouble Eros brings.[44] These troubles include both the pathos of

Psyche and the need to work imaginatively with the powers of erotic longing rather than taking them literally. The therapy that can hold these erotic torments without enactments or denial brings a transformation of soulmaking.

Different modalities approach love sickness variously. Some focus on the sexual side of Eros and relate the torments of love to a regressive Oedipal complex. The therapist's concern is with the dangers of acting out and falling into the triangular dynamic that the client is unconsciously attempting to resolve. Others get drawn into becoming better parents and attempting to compensate for the deprivations of their clients by showing their love. Transpersonal therapists may emphasize the spiritual side of Eros, sublimating any sexual feelings into desire for spiritual union. Clearly Eros has many sides.

However training centres attempt to support students, the arrival of erotic transference or erotic counter transference is nearly always a testing time. While there is a danger of taking the transference personally, there is also the danger of avoiding it by reading it as solely mother or father transference. While concern with boundaries is appropriate, if it is utilized as a defence against erotic attraction as if it were taboo, then the therapy can become arid, lifeless.

Haule makes the important distinction between the erotic as the energy of an interpersonal field where a sense of 'we-ness' comes forcefully to awareness, and *the sexual*, which involves 'an impulse to embody that *we-ness* in a genital manner'.[45] He cites Donleavy's critique of Rutter's classic warning on the dangers of the erotic field for therapists. As a therapist, whose own analyst did not flee from this encounter, Donleavy claims that failure to stay with the erotic tension by avoidance or acting out, disallows the potential for a healing image or experience to occur:

> With either choice the unconscious psychic part that was experienced through the desire or the fear stay still unconscious. If the tension can be held and the psychic part made conscious in each person, the couple will feel not the overwhelming need for physical merger but a psychic

resonance between them. This resonance will also be experienced as a new intrapsychic wholeness.[46]

Within the Re-Vision training, we explore erotic transference
first phenomenologically – is the experience hot, cold or indiffer-
ent? The importance is not just to give Eros a place in the consulting room but also to discriminate what sort of erotic feeling is
presenting itself. The myth of Psyche and Eros offers some significant clues as to how to read and work with the layers and differences within an erotic transference. While the experience of a hot
transference is difficult to miss and requires the therapeutic alliance to withstand the client's seduction and her/his frustration
at not having previously unmet needs consummated, a cool transference can cover a myriad of possibilities. It may include a detached or dissociated quality that defends against the dangers of
merger. The fear of intimacy is likely to emerge at the threshold
of mutuality (see the wheel model in Figure 5.1, above). At this
threshold, there can be a creative parallel between the dynamics
being played out in the client's outer relationships and what is
happening or not happening within the therapeutic relationship.
It may be that the client needs to explore intimacy within the relative safety of therapy before risking it with their partner.

The tendency of a therapist not practiced with playful intimacy
will be to shut down when the anxiety gets too much. Sedgwick
gives an honest account of attempting to work at this intense
threshold.[47] Not untypically for therapists, he thinks that the client
needs him to be able to hold the intensity. This is true within a
testing out phase of the therapeutic alliance, but holding onto this
as a requirement in a mutual phase is an avoidance of the therapist
surrendering their role and risking becoming vulnerable. This surrender can shift both therapist and client into a naked vulnerability, the meeting of soul with soul. The nakedness is not literal but
it feels just as exposing.

One of Re-Vision's principles is the tantric notion that, *we rise
by that by which we fall*. Counsellors and psychotherapists are often
falling, as in making mistakes. These may be subtle mistakes or
more significant misattunements, empathic failures that need to

be repaired. Such failures open the vulnerability of the therapist. Although the original mistake is unlikely to be conscious, its acknowledgement brings out the fallibility of the therapist. It is a sign that the therapist's power may need to be surrendered, their ego humbled. James Hillman says that *spirit* can see in the dark, while *soul* must feel its way. Soul feeling its way reflects an often awkward stumbling that reveals a crucial characteristic of the soul – its quality of vulnerability.

Vulnerability comes through wounding and opens a portal of healing. Along with personal wounds come cultural wounds; tears to the very fabric of what holds and allows us to comprehend each other. Implicit in this chapter is a commentary on cultural wounds to language, to the dry focus on efficiency and precision of meaning that science and economics have required. The cost of this cultural shift has been to the richness of ambiguity and a meaning that is not from knowledge about things but from presence. As Romanyshyn puts it, 'Psychological language is a way of speaking into the gap between meaning and the absence of meaning, a way of speaking of meaning as a presence that is haunted by absences'.[48]

'A way of speaking of meaning as a presence' already conjures up those encounters with soul that are difficult to language. And when we speak, the words may be haunted by absence, by the absence of the very experience we wished to communicate. And yet the awkward stumbling of our language, the vulnerable exposing of what is lost in our attempts, brings us present to each other in a humble revelation of soulful meeting.

To summarize this chapter on soulmaking, we have explored its need for

- A poetic speech that animates a therapeutic encounter.

- Deep pathos in the underworld out of reach of a colonizing ego.

- A longing of the heart that can hold intimacy and vulnerability.

I have attempted to show that 'scrape in the skin of knowing' mentioned in the opening Bateson quote, which allows the absence of soul to be made present. As our culture becomes increasing dissociated from live encounters and retreats to a virtual and domesticated world free from risk, the absence of soul becomes a cultural crisis. If psychotherapy goes down the same route towards efficiency, adjustment and commodification, then our sorrows will know no end. If the absence can be recognized as what is missing, then soulful approaches to psychotherapy can offer remedial repair to this tear in our cultural fabric through the soulmaking journey outlined above. For the presence of soul brings on the experience of joy and suffering, the delights of beauty and acceptance of ugliness. Soul wants to dwell in the vale of soul-making, as Keats called it, where it can be touched by grief and sadness at death, encounter terrible disappointments, experience the depth of melancholic dark blue, and yet where its longing for the beloved can bring a poignant rapture.

[1] Nora Bateson, 'Small Arcs of Larger Circles', at https://www.triarchypress.net/small-arcs.html (accessed 15 July 2018).

[2] James Hillman, *Healing Fiction* (Thompson, CT: Spring Publications, 1983).

[3] Hillman, *Healing Fiction*, pp. 17 – 18.

[4] Chris Robertson, 'Hungry Ghosts: Psychotherapy, control and the winds of homecoming', Self & Society 41, Issue 4 (2014), pp. 33 – 37.

[5] Jill Hayes, *Soul and Spirit in Dance Movement Psychotherapy* (London: Jessica Kingsley, 2013), p. 208.

[6] Carl Gustav Jung, *Modern Man in Search of a Soul* (London: Routledge, 1933).

[7] James Hillman, *Insearch: Psychology and Religion* (Irving, TX: Spring Publications, 1979).

[8] James Hillman, *Re-Visioning Psychology* (New York: Harper Perennial, 1975).

[9] Wilfred Bion, *Experience in Groups* (London: Tavistock, 1959).

[10] Morgan Farley, 'Clearing', *Heart Poems*, 25 August 2016, at https://janicefalls.wordpress.com/2016/08/25/clearing/ (accessed 26 July 2018).

[11] James Hillman, *Puer Papers* (Dallas, TX: Spring Publications, 1979), p. 115.

[12] James Hillman, *Myth of Analysis* (Evanston, IL: North Western University Press, 1997), p. 78.

[13] James Hillman, *Interviews* (Thompson, CT: Spring Publications, 1991), p. 100.

[14] David Abram, *Spell of the Sensuous* (New York: Vintage, 1996), p. 65.

[15] Chris Robertson, 'Dangerous Margins', Chapter 20 in *Vital Signs*, eds Mary-Jayne Rust and Nick Totton (London: Karnac, 2012).

[16] Robert Avens, 'Imagination is Reality', in *Western Nirvana in Jung, Hillman, Barfield and Cassirer* (Thompson, CT: Spring Publications, 1983).

[17] James Hillman, *Suicide and the Soul* (Thompson, CT: Spring Publications, 1978), p. 77.

[18] Winnicott said this at a Scientific Meeting of the British Psycho-Analytical Society, *circa* 1940.

[19] Tim Ingold, *On Being Alive* (London: Routledge, 2012). p. 64.

[20] Robertson, 'Dangerous Margins'.

[21] Carl Gustav Jung, *Psychology and Alchemy, The Collected Works*, Vol. 12 (New York: Princeton, 1953), p. 439.

[22] Carl Gustav Jung, *The Red Book: Liber Novus* (Philemon), ed. Sonu Shamdasani (New York: Norton, 2009),

[23] Hillman, *Re-Visioning Psychology*, p. 188.

[24] Hillman, *Re-Visioning Psychology*, p. 190.

[25] James Hillman, *Dream and the Underworld* (New York: HarperCollins, 1979), p. 47.

[26] Hillman, *Dream and the Underworld*.

[27] Hillman, *Dream and the Underworld*, p. 115.

[28] Leonard Shengold, *Soul Murder* (New York: Ballantine Books, 1990).

[29] Donald Kalsched, *The Inner World of Trauma: Archetypal Defenses of the Personal Spirit* (London: Routledge, 1996).

[30] Simone Weil, *Gravity and Grace*, trans. Emma Crawford (London: Routledge,1947/1963).

[31] David Rosen, *Transforming Depression* (York Beach, ME: Nicolas-Hays, 2002).

[32] James Hillman, *The Thought of the Heart and the Soul of the World* (Thompson, CT: Spring Publications, 1992), pp. 98 – 99.

[33] Keats Page, at http://academic.brooklyn.cuny.edu/english/melani/cs6/keatsltr.html (accessed 15 July 2018).

[34] Daryl Sharp, *The Secret Raven: conflict and transformation in the life of Franz Kafka* (Toronto: Inner City, 1980).

[35] Kalsched, *The Inner World of Trauma*.

[36] Hillman, *Puer Papers*, p. 232.

[37] Adolf Guggenbuhl-Craig, *Power in the Helping Professions* (Thompson, CT: Spring Publications, 1983).

[38] John Haule, *The Love Cure: Therapy Erotic and Sexual* (Thompson, CT: Spring Publications, 1996).

[39] Hakim Jami, *Yusuf and Zulaikha*, trans. David Pendlebury (London: Octagon Press, 1980).

[40] Dawn Freshwater and C. Robertson, *Emotions and Needs* (Buckingham: Open University Press, 1980).

[41] Hillman, *Myth of Analysis*, p. 95.

[42] Hillman, *The Thought of the Heart and the Soul of the World*.

[43] Joy Schaverien, *Desire and the Female Therapist* (London: Routledge, 1995).

[44] Thomas Warneke, 'Eros in body psychotherapy - A crucible of awakening, destruction and reparation', *Body, Movement and Dance in Psychotherapy*, 22 May 2018, at https://doi.org/10.1080/17432979.2018.1468822 (accessed 15 July 2018).

[45] Haule, *The Love Cure*, p. 55.

[46] Pamela Donleavy, *Analysis and Erotic Energies in The Interactive Field in Analysis*, ed. Murray Stein (Wilmette, IL: Chiron, 1995), p. 110.

[47] David Sedgewick, *The Wounded healer: Countertransference from a Jungian Perspective* (London: Routledge, 1994), p. 70.

[48] Robert Romanyshyn, *The Wounded Researcher: Research with Soul in Mind* (New Orleans, LA: Spring Publications, 2013), p. 29.

Chapter 6

Rediscovering Our Kinship with Nature: Ecological Issues in Psychotherapy
Joan Crawford

> Those who were sacred have remained so,
> holiness does not dissolve, it is a presence
> of bronze, only the sight that saw it
> faltered and turned from it.
> An old joy returns in holy presence.
> —Denise Levertov[1]

These lines from the poet Denise Levertov beautifully express the thrill we experience when our hearts open to the beauty and sacredness of the natural world. They also point to the limitations of our 'sight', when we are locked in our sense of separateness, what Alan Watts referred to as our 'skin encapsulated egos'. At the deepest level of our psyches, we are intimately interconnected and interdependent with the more-than and other-than human world. However, for most of us, our 'sight has faltered' and we have no awareness or appreciation of this natural state.

The inclusion of ecopsychology in the Re-Vision approach is a vital component for a range of reasons. It is an important development in widening the lens through which we see the psyche. Historically, psychotherapy focused on the individual psyche and the inner life of the client without paying too much attention to the context within which the individual was formed. Family therapy broadened the lens by exploring family systems and some therapies have begun to pay attention to larger social and cultural contexts. However, these developments remain within the realm of ego psychology. A transpersonal therapy is concerned with what happens when the ego is relegated to its rightful place as a useful ally, and the portals open to deeper dimensions. In such moments we may have flashes of insight about the meaning of our lives, encounter the numinous, or recognize that we are intimately interconnected and interdependent with everything that is. Such experiences bring with them a wonderful sense of both liberation and belonging. This perspective involves us in critiquing certain aspects of accepted psychological theory, which, in our view, serve to shore up the ego. We also pay attention to the cultural context in which we live, as the organs of contemporary society serve up a constant diet of fantasies and wish fulfilments that feed the ego. Whereas the ego is concerned with control, achieving goals, and getting ahead, ecology reveals to us a world in which things simply unfold in a glorious display without any intention of getting anywhere.

Returning to the Denise Levertov quote, the faltering of our sight has happened over millennia through a myriad of contributing factors. It is not within the scope of this chapter to explore all these factors, but to focus on a few significant ones: mind and body separated by religion; an immanent god replaced by a personalized transcendent one; the rise of patriarchy and the drive to conquer and subjugate others and the natural world; development of the scientific method and the control of the natural world that it gives rise to; the mechanistic view of the world as being composed of separate objects; the industrial revolution and the growth of urbanization; and the idea of progress which flows from many of these.

The cumulative impact of these and other influences have created a massive shift in our consciousness from an eco-centric view of the world to a human-centric or anthropocentric view of the world, also described as the 'empire of the ego'. We no longer recognize, as indigenous cultures did, and some still do, that we are an inextricable part of the web of life. Throughout much of human history, men and women experienced themselves as part of the larger community of the natural world and felt a sense of connection and kinship, not just with other people but with everything around them – trees, rocks, streams, a bird flying overhead, the distant mountains. For them, all of nature was alive and infused with the same spirit as themselves.

Matthew Fox has characterized this profound change in mind-set as a move from the web to the ladder.[2] In the words of Thomas Berry a species arrogance has developed in which humans see themselves as separate from, and superior to, nature; the world is a resource, to be used and exploited for our benefit.[3] This model of domination not only applies to nature, but has infected our thinking at every level, thereby creating hierarchies in all areas of life: men superior to women; whites superior to blacks; rationality superior to feeling and imagination; so called 'civilization' superior to indigenous communities. Life has become characterized by domination, competition and control. We are no longer deeply interconnected but set against both nature and each other in a constant drive to climb the ladder – the property ladder, the career ladder and, indeed, the spiritual ladder.

On an environmental level, this mindset has led to a world rife with perils: pollution of natural resources, loss of habitats, deforestation, depletion of the oceans, the potential cataclysm of climate change, to mention but a few. On a psychological level, we are witnessing the decimation of communities, proliferation of mental health problems and addictions, increasing isolation and lack of meaning.

At present, there are growing signs of a shift in the paradigm, partly fuelled by a sense of urgency about our current crisis, partly influenced by new understandings in the physical and natural sciences and, perhaps most importantly, by a recognition on the part of many people of the emptiness of much of modern living and a longing to find deeper and more meaningful relationships and connections, both with each other and with the world.

A story of a whaler in California is a particularly moving and telling illustration of what might be described as a revelatory experience, in which the individual's sense of herself or himself of the world is profoundly altered. He and his fellow fishermen feared grey whales. Their practice was to kill baby whales in order to draw their mothers in close, and the whales fought back ferociously. One day a local fisherman, despite his fear, and for some inexplicable reason, reached out to touch a whale near his boat.

I don't know what compelled me to reach out my hand. The moment I touched the whale for the first time I felt something incredible. I lost my fear. I was amazed, it was like breaking through some kind of invisible wall. And I kept touching. That moment I compare with when my first child was born. It left a deep impression in my heart.[4]

In that moment, the fisherman broke through to an awareness of his deep interconnection with the whales, to a profoundly different state of consciousness. When commentators talk about a new consciousness and a need to reconnect with a sense of embeddedness in the natural world, some construe this as a need to return to what they would term, pejoratively, a primitive life style. The work of the philosopher and poet Owen Barfield is illuminating in this context. Barfield outlined three stages in the evolution of consciousness: original participation, withdrawal of participation and final participation. In the first phase, human beings participated in an enchanted universe through myth, poetry, dance, music, fertility, and nature. The withdrawal of participation corresponds to 'the ladder' of the modern era; our connection with the natural world has been broken and we are trapped inside ourselves. He described final participation as a stage when the 'best of each era will combine and work together: the prerational, the rational, and the transrational. In this consciousness, we can now enjoy intuitive and body knowledge, along with rational critique and deeper synthesis, thus encouraging both intelligent and heartfelt participation with our whole heart, soul, mind and strength'.[5]

Barfield's stages of consciousness accords with Ken Wilber's thoughts on the Pre/Trans fallacy. He points out that each stage of growth in individual consciousness transcends the previous one, but that it also includes its predecessor. 'To transcend mind in Spirit is not to lose mind or destroy mind but merely to include mind in the higher order wholeness of the superconscient. What is negated is the exclusivity of mind; what is preserved is the capacity of mind'.[6] By the same token, moving from the ego phase to the trans-ego phase is not a question of letting go of the ego, but rather retaining the functions of ego while letting go of its limitations. The model below illustrates the parallels in stages and consciousness, both individual and societal. Ken Wilber's model is linear, implying a ladder to a higher order trans-ego place as a goal to attain, whereas the Re-Vision model is cyclical, challenging this growth model. In the individual, the unconscious will unfailingly throw up new material, which necessitates a return to earlier stages to rework that material. The model implies that progression never proceeds smoothly and that there are regressions as well as progressions in both individuals and societies.

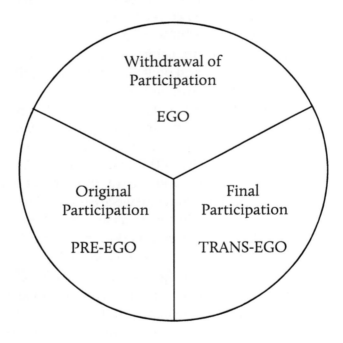

Figure 6.1. Stages of Consciousness.

Whether we are conscious of it or not, I believe many of us are caught between the old and the new. The ladder mentality is deeply ingrained in us all but, at the same time, we are suffering the effects of it and are searching in our lives for something richer and more deeply fulfilling. I want to look now at the ways in which issues relating to this discussion may arise in therapy, the approaches we might take to those issues, and the ways in which therapy itself, far from helping to heal the splits, may sometimes contribute to their persistence.

The remarkable statement below by the psychiatrist Ronald Searles, made almost 60 years ago, still largely holds true today.

> The nonhuman environment,... is, by implication, considered as irrelevant to human personality development, and to the development of psychiatric illness, as though human life were lived out in a vacuum – as though the human race were alone in the universe, pursuing individual and collective destinies in a homogenous matrix of nothingness, a background devoid of form, color, and substance.[7]

Significantly, D.W. Winnicott's famous phrase, the 'Facilitating Environment', referred to the mother but made no mention of the larger physical environment. For him, 'the holding environment' was the mother, or the mothering person of early childhood – the quality of her voice, the contours of her body, the rhythm of her breathing, the sensation of her touch. But the infant is born into not only a social context but also an ecological context. She is aware not only of human contact but also the touch of the breeze on her skin, the chirping of birds, the smell of grass, the sun reflected on water. The awakening of sensuousness, pleasure and delight in the infant most likely results from the intermingling of the mother and the world she inhabits. And, in the event that the mother is non-responsive, impinging, or harsh, the natural world may provide vital compensations. In groups I run, I invite participants to picture themselves as young children connecting to a favourite place in nature, a creature or a pet and to explore the experience in their imaginations. What is striking in the feedback is that the connections are experienced as mutual: as a child they felt loved as well as loving, they felt soothed and comforted. Some participants have reported that they felt nature played a critical role in saving them from despair. In client work it is helpful to bring in this dimension at the outset, inquiring about their relationships with nature. As well as helping them to remember positive experiences, these recollections can point to ways in which the individual may resource themselves in the present.

In the infant's contact both with the mother and the larger environment, it is the permeability of his or her boundaries which allows them to revel in sensual experience. Developmental theory emphasizes the importance of establishing strong enough boundaries to protect us from being overwhelmed and losing a sense of self. However, if our boundaries are too rigid, we separate ourselves both from the world and from others and, in the process, cut ourselves off from potential nourishment.

> Ideally, we need to develop semi permeable boundaries, that are neither too rigid or too diffuse, to build enough of a membrane around ourselves to be able to function within a culture and at the same time allow the membrane to be permeable/receptive enough to sensation, feeling and communion. Our culture's insistence on independence, mastery and competition has led to the popularity of a psychology that emphasizes only the first aspect of the child's task.[8]

This is the goal of separation and individuation, the presumed requirement for becoming a mature adult. It does, however, come at a tremendous price. In emphasizing the separate self we lose sight of our inherent intimate connection with the world, and the richness that such connection can gift us. In our skin-encapsulated ego we are impervious to the sensuousness and the beauty that surrounds us. Our relationship with the more-than-human and other-than-human world is essentially an erotic one. Eros is the force that endlessly connects and creates. We live in a world of shared relationships, not only with each other but also with everything we encounter.

It is often through experiences of beauty that our eyes are opened to the world and we are brought into immediate sensual relationship with everything around us. Even if we are stuck in our heads, beauty can startle us and take our breath away as we gaze in wonder. In such moments the assumed boundary between inner and outer dissolves and we experience moments of communion.

This is the anima mundi of the ancients, in which there is no separation between our souls and the soul of the world. Experiences like these engender a sense of mystery and meaning, profoundly altering people's perceptions and creating a new zest for life.

My own epiphany came in a wood awash with primroses. My first response on seeing them was to think, 'Oh, aren't they pretty', but gradually I began to notice the detail and particularity of the flowers – their delicate yellow colour, their crinkly petals, they way they peaked out from under a log, their pert quality. I also became increasingly aware of the woods around me – a leaf fluttering in the breeze, a shaft of light filtering through the canopy, the individual and differing notes of birdsong rather than just a melodic background. All of my senses were alive and quivering. I became intensely aware that everything was animated, alive, in motion, rhythmic, dancing.

I was not only intensely aware of the world around me but had a sense that the world was intensely aware of me: that we were in dialogue, intimate communication, intercourse. The breeze was caressing my skin, earth was cushioning my body, the primroses were winking at me. The quality of each thing I related to seemed to set up a reverberation in me; the soul in it found an echo in my soul, my being mingled with theirs; I was pervaded by them. It was an experience of profound intimacy.

In such moments we are caught unawares and 'surprised by joy' in the words of Wordsworth.[9] But we can also intentionally develop a more receptive mode of relating to the world: by shifting our usual sense of consciousness from the head to the heart; by consciously softening our boundaries; and by cultivating attention and alertness. As in all meaningful relationships, a certain vulnerability and openness to being touched is necessary. These are experiences of deep intimacy in which our hearts are deeply moved, and they are also the experiences which so many of us lack in our lives. As James Hillman comments:

> We might be relieved of the desperation for intimacy, the transference clutch, the narrow personalisation of love, the fear of loneliness. Intimacy occurs when we live in a

world of particular, concrete events, noticeable for what
William James called their "eachness". The joyful scrutiny
of detail, the intimacy of each with each such as lovers
know. A world without soul offers no intimacy.[10]

In modern culture, our drive for intimacy and erotic connection is largely confined to sexuality and is often driven by feelings
of emptiness. What we have seen from the above discussion is that
these experiences are gifted to us if we allow ourselves to be open
to them. Stepping outside my normal abstinence from giving advice, I encourage clients to be aware of the infinite sensuousness
of existence, the delight and pleasure that arises from smell, taste,
touch, sight and hearing. Rather than walking down the street
with their heads stuck in their phones and listening to music
pounding through their earphones, they might notice the sensation of the sun on their face, the wind ruffling their hair, the
clouds drifting in the sky. In some instances, I may suggest a practice of visiting the same place every day and noting the minute details of each thing, being alert to the small changes they observe.
The intention is to foster a degree of receptivity which makes the
possibility of finding true intimacy in all realms of life much more
likely. As part of the Re-Vision approach, we don't see the work as
being confined to the therapy room. Practices done between sessions can be important in deepening the work.

In his book, *Borderlands*, Jungian analyst Jerome Bernstein recounts his experience working with people who are particularly
permeable and sensitive to what they pick up from the environment. Initially he viewed these clients through the classical lens
of psychotherapy and understood their responses as a form of projection, i.e., seeing parts of nature representing parts of themselves. One particular client was telling him in great distress about
two cows being hauled into a truck for slaughter. She became fu-
rious when he interpreted her experience on a symbolic level and
shouted at him, 'It's the cows, stupid!'. He gradually changed his
view as a result of a number of similar presentations, and came to
the conclusion that these clients were carrying something for the
collective. He uses the term, 'The Borderland Personality', to de-

note people whose unconscious is particularly attuned to the violence we do to the more-than and other-than human world, and suffer as a result. They are often seen by others as mad, are described as over-sensitive, and have often been ridiculed. The intense nature of their presentations can be understood as compensatory, taking an extreme form in direct contrast to the collective indifference and cruelty of the prevailing culture. Conventionally, it would be easy to see their responses as a result of personal trauma; but whilst many have experienced abuse in their childhoods, many have not.

> For some of the Borderland individuals I have cited here, although they acknowledge the trauma portal as their initial access to the Borderland, they are adamant in their insistence that their Borderland existence not be seen as an extension of, or attached to, their traumatic experience – ie. pathologized... *They do not want it pathologized.* When it is pathologized, it feels like a profanation of something sacred.[11]

He was particularly struck by the dreams these clients brought. Dreams from a number of them had such strikingly similar themes, 'as if the ecological unconscious is speaking to western culture through the medium of the dreams'.[12] He cites the following dream:

> I dreamed I was on a beach. Children in their swimsuits, wearing sunglasses and cotton hats, were digging sand with small shovels and several bathers lay on blankets taking in the sun. All around them were hundreds of dead seals, which had been washed up on the shore, some in huge piles. The children and adults were acting as if they were completely unaware of the dead animals right next to them. In my dream, I was the only witness. Standing in front of the stacked-up bodies of seals I began to plead with the people. Don't you know, I called out to them, 'unless you do something now, what is happening to the seals will happen to you too'.[13]

From an ecological point of view, the significance of the dream couldn't be clearer. But if you aren't looking through that lens, no doubt other interpretations could be made from a symbolic point of view, i.e., the seals representing aspects of the dreamer's psyche. Improbable as this may seem, it happens. When Buddhist scholar and environmental activist Joanna Macy was expressing her grief about the destruction of the wilderness, her therapist treated her grief as a private neurosis, interpreting that 'the bulldozers were symbolic of her own libido and that her distress sprang from fear of her own sexuality'.[14]

When the more-than-human or the other-than-human world appears in clients' experiences or dreams it is important to honour them in their own right. Viewing them as merely representations of our instincts disrespects them, treating them only as servants to our personal process. The dream above carries a disturbing message from the ecological unconscious. It is important to be alert to possible communications from the web, even when the dreams are not as clear as this one.

It is essential to validate the experience of clients who present with troubling concerns about what is happening in the world. They may be reluctant to reveal some of their responses, given the ways in which they have been seen, and will quickly sense scepticism or judgment on the part of the therapist. At the same time, it is also necessary to work with personal pain. It is not an either/or choice, but steering a course between the two can be challenging. It is important to begin with validating clients' experience in order to build trust and to wait for the opportunity to explore more personal issues, if relevant. A client of mine had been watching a television programme about a place where wounded animals were dumped and left to die. She was extremely distressed and tearful about their plight. I empathized with her distress and agreed that it was heart breaking and symptomatic of our society's cruelty, and gradually she calmed down. With some clients I might have asked them whether there was some action they might want to take but as this client was a super 'do-er', I felt it was important in that moment that she experienced her grief. I was also aware of the client's history of abandonment but felt an interpretation, at the time, would be inappropriate. I was able to bring it in later in the therapy when the alliance was well established, but was careful to emphasize that a personal view did not in any way invalidate her original response.

Borderland personalities appear to have little or no choice about their extreme responses to what they see and feel is happening to the world. For many people, an awareness of the crisis of the planet probably exists just below the threshold of consciousness and they may choose not to think about it or to push it out of awareness. In groups I have run, I invite people to speak to what they find most distressing about what is happening in the world. Although there is an element of choice in those who attends these groups (i.e., they are already troubled), the invitation is often met with discomfort and anxiety. I believe there a cultural taboo against asking people to confront these issues directly. What I imagine is happening is that people are anxious that if they let themselves feel their pain for the world, they will be incapacitated by it, as well as being overcome with feelings of guilt for their part in our current crisis, and that they will experience disabling feelings of powerlessness. As participants begin to voice what pains them, the atmosphere changes: tears flow, there is often anger, expressions of helplessness and despair, but also a huge feeling of relief. Feelings that have been kept under wraps are given expression and people are given permission to grieve. And just as grief work is a process whereby bereaved people unblock their feelings by grieving the loss of someone they love, by the same token, unblocking our feelings about the threatened loss of our planet liberates something within us. Joanna Macy expresses this beautifully:

> The workshops taught me more than I could ever have imagined. The thousands of people I have worked with in church basements, community centres and classrooms have revealed to me the power, size and beauty of the human heart. They have revealed that pain for the world touches each of us, and that this pain is rooted in caring... By recognising our capacity to suffer with the world, we

dawn to the wider dimensions of being. There is still pain, but also a lot more. There is wonder, even joy as we come home to our mutual belonging – and there is a new kind of power.[15]

If clients bring these concerns to therapy, apart from encouraging them to talk and honouring their feelings, I think it is important to share our own struggles with overwhelm and fear. There is an epidemic of loneliness in our society and this pain, like any other pain, cannot be borne alone. When we sit with our clients and include our mutual grief and their sorrow, they can find ways to tolerate it and, possibly, come through to a sense of what it might be theirs to do in the world. It is less straightforward if the client isn't conscious of their concerns, although it may be an unacknowledged dimension of their struggles. The right question or comment at the right time may reveal an element of distress that they have failed to recognize. Mary-Jayne Rust provides a telling example:

> Last year a client of mine, who came into therapy about relationship difficulties, revealed that she and her partner (both 30-somethings) spent their entire leisure time drinking and taking drugs. This was not a problem, she said; all her friends did likewise. We circled around this for a while. I was baffled as I could not find the real despair and anger underneath this wipe out. In the midst of a session, I threw in a wild card: 'What do you feel about the future?' She replied, 'We're completely fucked.' She talked about our global crisis at length, and she spontaneously made the link to her drinking, saying, 'We may as well go down having a good time.'[16]

Many observers commenting on the state of modern society identify a sense of meaninglessness, emptiness and aloneness which pervades the lives of many people. Consumerism, the search for status, addictions, the pursuit of affluence, the cult of celebrity, fascination with technology and the lack of community and social isolation, to mention but a few, are rife. All these disorders populate our therapy rooms; our method, as therapists, is to search for the cause of these disorders in the personal history of clients. Classically, we believe that addictions, the inability to form meaningful relationships, or obsessions with achievement and success, all arise from some form of deprivation or deficiency in clients' childhoods. Whilst there are clearly benefits arising from this approach it also has its limitations. What is missing from this perspective is an awareness of, and attention to, the collective nature of these problems. We are all deeply influenced by the dominant culture in which we live – we soak it up daily through the media, advertising, shopping malls, the news and much of our education system. We are bombarded with images to which we are encouraged to aspire: to be the most successful, most beautiful, most exotic, most exceptional, most sexually alluring and so on.

An exercise I do in groups is designed to bring participants to an awareness of the way in which we are all affected or, more appropriately infected, by the pervasive influence of such images. Participants are presented with a number of cards, each one naming certain attitudes, beliefs and behaviours of our prevailing culture, e.g., need to be special, desire for material possessions, pursuit of affluence, quest for the exotic and so on. Participants are invited to notice which one/s speak to them of their own reactions, something they are familiar with about themselves, or which ones they shun. After some consideration, they choose one and are then invited to explore the ways in which this predilection functions in their lives, their degree of attachment to it, and what they imagine they would lose if they were to let go of it.

In the process, participants sometimes realize how ephemeral the satisfactions that arise from ego-based pursuits are; although we get a temporary hit from our latest purchase or our moment of glory, it rapidly fades. Each hit has to be more powerful than the last, thereby strengthening the craving. In terms of what they might lose, more often than not it is what the thing symbolizes, rather than the thing itself, that matters: they would be seen as less successful, less attractive, less interesting, less worth knowing by others and so on. So much of what we seek is for narcissistic gratification rather than the inherent satisfaction and enjoyment that the objects of our desire might provide. Our consumer society also inculcates a sense of entitlement, a feeling that we have a right to whatever we want, which reinforces the behaviour.

Although we are talking about the *collective* characteristics of society we can only access these through *the personal*, our own attitudes, beliefs and behaviours. The exercise is not designed to make people feel guilty but to help them recognize the degree to which we are caught in something over which we, seemingly, have no control. At its best, it relieves some of the feeling of guilt. It is also deeply challenging to really own those beliefs and predilections and to look closely at how they control behaviour. The first step, as with any unconscious identification, is to recognize it and, perhaps to forgive ourselves for the ways in which we contribute to the current crisis. This recognition may help to loosen the grip of those attachments and open the door to new attitudes and fresh responses. It may also become apparent that the challenge to a sense of narcissistic entitlement engenders refusal and anger.

In client work, although we work predominantly with the personal level of disorders, there can be a point at which it is helpful to widen the context. For example, when working with a food addiction, we can point to the hunger that drives our society on so many levels: our voracity that is consuming the world's natural resources; our refusal, as a society, to accept any limits to the exploitation of the Earth; the affluent world facing a crisis of obesity whilst much of the world's population still doesn't have enough to eat. Clearly, it is a matter of judgment whether such interventions could be helpful to the client or simply plunge them deeper into guilt, and whether they are delivered in a way that conveys that we are all implicated in this predicament. In my experience, seeing their struggles within a larger context sometimes brings a helpful perspective, taking them out of their narrow preoccupation with themselves and leading to salutary remorse and, sometimes, a spur to action.

I have tried to emphasize throughout this chapter the vital importance of our interconnection and interdependence with the more-than-human or the other-than-human world. 'An ecosystemic therapy approach means taking the view that each of us is created by the web, at the same time as we co-create the web. Our relationship with all the features in our environment is a *mutual* one: we are shaping them as they are shaping us'.[17] As therapists we are familiar with the idea of the synergetic field, whereby the unconscious of therapist and client between them create a field, which on the one hand is the product of their interactions and, on the other, becomes a palpable presence which in turn affects both therapist and client. Ecosystemic therapy expands the idea of the field to include everything – a bird at the window, a shaft of sunlight, a bee buzzing in the room. And, as we put attention on the manifestations of the field, such as bodily sensations, an intrusive thought, a spontaneous image, we can allow them (it) to come into focus through our attention and muse about what meanings they might have. A beautiful example is provided by Mary-Jayne Rust:

> I remember a very moving moment in a session when my client was unable to speak for some time. I could tell she was feeling distressed and cut off, and I had tried several times to build a bridge with words, but the gap between us remained. Then, in the same moment, we both glanced down to see the tiniest of spiders weaving a web between our arms. We grinned at each other, speechless with wonder, making a deep connection without the need for words. In subsequent sessions we spoke of how the spider's web was an affirmation about trusting the connecting processes of life in that most difficult moment.[18]

In my own practice, I had been working for a long time with a client who had deep attachment to feeling victimized. We had approached the issue from numerous angles but it just didn't seem to shift. On one occasion we were just coming to the end of a piece of work in which he was confronted with his stubborn holding onto this identification, despite his conscious desire to let go of it. As he wrestled with the conflict, an image of a tiny fissure in a rock popped into my head. At the same moment, a leaf from the fig tree in my counselling room detached itself from its stem and gently floated to the floor. We were both arrested by the sight and stared at it, and then at each other, in silent amazement. Interestingly, we never spoke about it but, in retrospect, that moment seems to have been a turning point in his struggle. This might be understood as synchronicity, or alternatively, as a message from the web. There was something about the graceful and effortless fall of the leaf, which could be construed as a reassurance about the outcome of letting go.

Although these are particularly dramatic examples, occurrences like these happen more often than we might imagine. It is a question of allowing our attention to be open to them and being willing to believe that they could have some meaning. It may be that what catches our attention relates to some half formed idea in our minds. The light fading in the room may help to focus our thinking about a shadow aspect of the client and to confirm an intuition.

I have looked at a range of ways in which ecological issues may arise in therapy and the ways in which we may address them. It is more a question of having a particular perspective that alerts us to their presence, rather than having a series of procedures to follow. Above all, it is not about imposing our views on clients, but helping them to see how the broader issues may be a thread that runs though their personal concerns. If we look back at the three-phased model I presented earlier in the chapter, it may be that a client experiencing their intimate connection with, and participation in, the web of life allows them momentarily to cross the threshold from egoic concerns to a deeper and more fulfilling, soulful sense of life. And in this process they may be contributing to the larger shift in consciousness that Barfield suggested was possible.

At the time he was writing, Barfield would not have had the awareness we now have of the threats to the planet and the potential cataclysm we face. This awareness engenders in many of us an enormous sense of urgency, the feeling that we must do something to save the world. Much of the discussion of environmental issues focuses around whether we have reached a tipping point, whether we have enough time to turn things around, whether this action or that action will make a difference and so on. In other words, how can we control what is happening? Although actions are clearly necessary, this raises is a striking paradox in relation to both therapy and ecology. A certain amount of our work in therapy is helping people see that they don't have the sort of control over their lives that they think they have, or believe they would like to have, in order to gain the state they imagine would provide the satisfaction they are searching for.

By the same token, as therapists it is vital that we know that we cannot control the process of therapy, i.e., make things happen. Acceptance of this bald fact, although difficult, can lead clients to relax their drivenness and to lead their lives more spontaneously; it can also lead therapists to function more creatively. It is also important to recognize that ecosystems aren't trying to get somewhere; they are simply unfolding through myriad connections, exchanges, adaptations and transformations. These understandings have an enormous relevance for the larger society: many of the actions that are taken to try and control what is happening, far from solving the problems, only serve to exacerbate them.

Nick Totton cites Hardt and Negri's image of an orchestra with no conductor, in which the network of players 'produce and innovate together, without the imposition of a conductor's central authority'.

> This is the basis for an ecological society, founded on ecological consciousness. And, paradoxically, there is little that we as individuals can do to create it deliberately! If it is going to come into existence, then it must be already brewing, already cooking in many thousand of places around the planet; slowly assembling itself out of millions of local acts of creativity and resistance.[19]

As I come to the end of this chapter, I gaze out the window and my eye is caught by a goldfinch that has darted onto the birdfeeder. Its red crest glistens in the sun as it pecks at the seeds, glancing about with alert watchfulness. The next minute it streaks away displaying its black and golden wings. My heart lifts and a feeling of innocence pervades me. 'An old joy returns in holy presence'.[20]

1 Denise Levertov, *Poems 1960 – 1967* (New York: New Directions Books, 1983), p. 23.

2 Matthew Fox, *A Spirituality Named Compassion: Uniting Mystical Awareness with Social Justice* (Rochester, VT: Inner Traditions, 1999), pp. 37 – 65.

3 Thomas Berry, *The Great Work: Our Way into the Future* (New York: Bell Tower, 1999), p. 89.

4 James William Gibson, *A Reenchanted World* (New York: Metropolitan Books, 2009), pp. 43 – 44.

5 Owen Barfield, *Saving the Appearances* (New York: Harcourt Brace, 1957), cited in Richard Rohr, *Immortal Diamond: The Search for our True Self* (London: Society for Promoting Christian Knowledge, 2013), p. 116.

6 Ken Wilber, 'The Pre/Trans Fallacy', *ReVision* 3, no. 2 (Fall 1980), p. 5.

7 Harold Searles, *The Nonhuman Environment In Normal Development and in Schizophrenia* (New York: International Universities Press, 1960), p. 3.

8 Anita Barrows, *The Ecopsychology of Child Development*, in Theodore Roszak, Mary E. Gomes and Allen D. Kanner, eds, *Ecopsychology* (San Francisco, CA: Sierra Club Books, 1995), p. 105.

9 William Wordsworth, *Poems 1815* (General Books LLC, 2009), cited in *The Oxford Dictionary of Quotations* (Oxford: Oxford University Press, 1979), p. 582.

10 James Hillman, *The Thought of the Heart and the Soul of the World* (Woodstock, CT: Spring Publications, 1981), p. 120.

11 Jerome S. Bernstein, *Living in the Borderland: The Evolution of consciousness and the challenge of healing trauma* (London and New York: Routledge, 2005), p. 94.

12 Bernstein, *Living in the Borderland*, p. 76.

13 Bernstein, *Living in the Borderland*, p. 76.

14 Joanna Macy, 'Working Through Environmental Despair', in Theodore Roszak, Mary E. Gomes and Allen D. Kanner, eds, *Ecopsychology* (San Francisco, CA: Sierra Club Books, 1995), p. 244.

15 Macy, 'Working Through Environmental Despair', p. 251.

16 Mary-Jayne Rust, 'Climate on the couch: unconscious processes in relation to the environmental crisis', *Psychotherapy and Politics International* 6, no. 3 (2008), pp. 157 – 170; pp. 162 – 163.

17 Nick Totton, *Wild Therapy: Undomesticating inner and outer worlds* (Ross-on-Wye: PCCS Books, 2011), p. 187.

18 Mary-Jayne Rust, 'Why and how do therapists become ecotherapists?', in L. Buzzell and C. Chalquist, eds, *Ecotherapy with nature in Mind* (San Francisco, CA: Sierra Club Books, 2009), p. 43.

19 Totton, *Wild Therapy*, p. 211.

20 Levertov, *Poems 1960 – 1967* p.23

Chapter 7

Madness in the Method
Jo-Ann Roden

> Pathologising is homeopathic, like cures like. There must
> be madness in the method if the method would reach
> the madness.[1]

The initial conditions of a dynamic system play a significant role in developing the system over time. Beginnings matter for a system's formation in the way that acorns materialize into the trees they will become. A beginning will implicate its end.[2] With this in mind, an ethically responsible training needs to be mindful of the context within which psychotherapy students are initiated. Training methods matter, because they model the method being taught, and plant the seed values and root metaphors that will unfold over time. The Hillman quote above suggests that in order to reach 'the madness', we need to include a drop of madness in the method. For trainee psychotherapists this means giving a place to the potential chaos of the unknown and the unknowable; to accept that all is in flux. It's a lot to ask. So we hold the archetype of the wounded healer as central, thereby giving our own 'psychopathology', or madness, a place.

In this chapter I'm attempting to disclose something of how beginnings matter in becoming a psychotherapist. How the non-rational plays an inherent part in this process, up to and including an acceptance of disorder in the system. So this chapter will *not* be reasonably argued and may feel disordered to read and impressionistic in style. This, for me, reflects the struggle: how to make sense of what cannot readily be made sense of. This chapter aims to describe what, from my perspective, makes the Re-Vision training method so valuable.

A personal myth

The root metaphor of depth psychology: mythology presents pathology; pathology, mythology. We require both to grasp either.[3]

A dream from twenty years ago...

> *I'm in a theatre. It's a grand place and I'm viewing from the upper circle. There are characters on the stage who seem shady. The backdrop is a huge black curtain. I am drawn to this backdrop. I'm pulled in and as I hit the black curtain, I disappear. I land, finding myself in an African landscape. It's a dusty village with red earth. The air is warm but the sun is on its way down. As I begin to take some steps into the village, an elderly man approaches me. He is not African. I realize he looks a bit like Carl Jung. He hands me an essay I'd written about my grandfather saying that it's getting there but it still needs more work.*

My grandfather, who lived and worked in Africa, took his own life when my father was an adolescent. My father's maternal grandfather had also committed suicide. My father disclosed these truths to me when I was an adolescent. As time has gone on, I've realized the significance of trans-generational trauma in my own story, particularly around connection and severance of being. It seems that healing in the present can enable a retrograde healing of the past. The dream above alerted me to the depth to which my grandfather's story was working its way through me. After this night visitation, I felt an increasingly visceral connection with the thread to my ancestors. I began to make sense of my life differently. As a child, I was drawn to images of beginnings and darkness: the night sky, dark poetry, music and comedy, cosmological concepts, the birth of stars, black holes. Latterly, through my psychotherapy training, I've found relief in the imagery of the underworld, and noticed that what has worked its way through my personal psyche is often a reflection of occurrences in the collective psyche. Dreams provide evidence for this. Rationally, I struggled to explain the mechanism of how this inner/outer parallel could happen, and the immense power that imagery, wordlessness and non-verbal states can have in making sense of experience.

Soulful psychopathology

Out of psyche – pathos – logos came the meaning of suffering of the soul or souls suffering of meaning.[4]

The word 'psychopathology' can be broken down into psyche (of soul), pathos (of suffering and being moved) and logos (of meaning/place). With Hillman's definition, we are urged to give soul-suffering a place. This is a definition which, in contrast to the mainstream medical usage of the term, delineates both the study of mental illness and is a descriptive term used to denote symptoms of mental illness. The medical model assumes that something is wrong. We would rather recognize psychopathology as the client's cry, 'What's wrong with me?' The question suggests there could be a solution that will take away their symptoms and this is the root of problem-solving or corrective psychologies.

Soulful psychopathology holds that symptoms which suggest mental illness to some are a necessary development in the soul's journey. In Hillman's sense, pathologizing is: the psyche's autonomous ability to create illness, fantasy, morbidity, disorder, abnormality and suffering and to experience life through this afflicted perspective using different lenses (mythical, religious, artistic etc.) whilst maintaining another view which differs from this and is psychological.[5] Pathologizing is not wrong but necessary. Pathologizing involves purposes that offer themselves in a distorted form. Instead of pathologizing in the medical model way, we could be asking: What might these symptoms be saying to us? What *is* unfolding for the individual and for the collective?

By giving a place to our darker, more disordered aspects, we are taking the being of Psyche seriously. When for example, we have a client who presents with what can be thought of as borderline symptoms (e.g., the terror of abandonment depression, and a tendency to idealize that easily tips into hatred), we can explore the meaning of these as though they are an expression of both an individual and a cultural complex.

One way to widen the context from a narrow view of psychopathology as the meaning of suffering is to ask instead, what is this 'suffering of' meaning? This context is not asking for explanations but is the work involved in staying with the pain of wounding – potentially transforming how we feel in the present through meaning making. It also helps us to make sense of the darkness in our personal and ancestral histories. So, for instance, working with myth, dream and image can help us to connect with the despair of our ancestors in ways that are bearable, to find a deep resonance for the suffering of others in the present, and to connect with a sense of the kind of future we are all creating for those yet to come. To participate in a soulful training is to allow these personal questions a place that reconnects us with collective struggles. This is part of what allows us to hope that there can be a place where we can make sense of our suffering – a place we can call 'home'. Such a homecoming is coming home to oneself as a call of soul.

The remainder of this chapter attempts to describe some ingredients of the relationally soulful method that has emerged through Re-Vision's thirty-year history.

Remembering and Dismembering

In order to move away from our ego-centred preoccupations, the training at Re-Vision is offered as a *soul-centred* approach. Trainees are invited to be preoccupied with the movements of psyche in both her creative *and* destructive aspects. We are invited to attune to Soul's whispers even if we hear what at first seems like madness. Images of dark mother Goddesses come to mind, such as Kali or Erishkegal. The heart of a soulful approach includes a process of dissolution or de-integration, dissolving or dis-membering our hardened outer surfaces, to reveal a softer or more permeable core.

In order to arrive at a new story and different landscape, we dis-member our constructed understanding of our personal story (and those of clients) and re-member it in the wider context of collective story. One of the beauties inherent in a soul-centred approach lies in *how* this dis-membering and re-membering occurs. Re-Vision offers an integrative approach that is not solely about understanding how differing models hang together, but is one that prepares all students by inviting them in to a deeper exploration of their own wounding. Hillman reminds us that our wounds are the mothers and fathers of our destiny. He urges us to move away from a thinking that is based solely on the 'parental fallacy', which depends on 'one way, vertical causality from larger to smaller'. So, for example, in order to explore narcissism, students are invited to come in to closer relationship with their own narcissistic wounds.

In the first stage of the training, students work with their own stories. They encounter a developmental cycle as they move through the foundation year and reconnect with the Soul's Journey of their own lives. Our relational method of 'inside out' learning reveals itself through experience via right hemispheric channels such as bodily sensations, dream images and noticing synchronistic occurrences. These are given a place alongside the integration of ideas, using left hemispheric verbal and analytic means.

Falling in to the universe

> Out beyond ideas of wrongdoing
> and right doing there is a field.
> I'll meet you there.
> When the soul lies down in that grass
> the world is too full to talk about.
> —Rumi[6]

One year ago I dreamt the following...

A massive earthquake has devastated my house and the entire town that I live in. Everything has been reduced to blackened rubble. I'm away from home and need to find my way back over vast yawning crevices that have opened up around me. I find a pair of red running shoes. When I put them on, they allow me somehow to run through the chaos.

As I find my street, and see that my house has disappeared,
I notice a run-down old shack that has appeared close by. I
find my way inside and sitting at a table by a window, is a
smiling baby. She is blackened too, but is alive, and in front
of her on the tabletop is a pot of ointment that she is lovingly
smoothing into her skin. I know she is showing me the way.

This dream offered me an image of what needed to be done in my own relational sphere. It offered up an image of the fault line in my inner world, and an image of the way through, and guided me back into therapy and back into my paternal wounds. The dream presents a mirror of my worlds – pointing both to something yet to emerge and to the deep roots of my ancestral past. As above so below.[7] What was stirring in the depths of my being was a level of relational disruption that my upper-world existence was in denial of.

A key element throughout the training, and the workings of the organization, is relational contact, with all the creative struggle this throws up. Being in relationship is messy and at times challenging, but how could we exist outside of it? Being *is* relational. More psychoanalytic models have eventually taken this on board and moved away from instinct theory to a more relational theory of self/ego. It is now widely understood that babies are born already within a complex state of relationship with mother (and so, with the world).

Etymologically, the word is derived from the Latin *relatio*, denoting to 'bring back', and the Medieval English suffix *ship*, denoting a property or state of being (itself derived from the Frisian Dutch-Germanic *schip* denoting 'water born vessel'). Other references relate to a connecting shape or form. Images form in my mind of movement across watery spaces, of ships that connect lands and peoples, that are part of trading, part of warring. There is shadow here too, with, for example, the dark murderous history of slave trading and the extracting and plundering of natural resources.

Today, some may take it for granted that we can all easily make connections and be in relationship. Since the advent of the Internet and with the rise of social media, there is an increasing possibility for connection. Yet perhaps this sort of contact is not really making the soulful connections we all long for. Some would say that the rise of cyber interconnectivity raises anxiety levels to narcissistic heights, with a relentless focus on both how we are seen, and how we are seeing others.

Maybe the word relationship can be somewhat misguiding. Donald Winnicott spoke to this with his famous assertion, 'there's no such thing as a baby'.[8] We are always, and necessarily, in relationship with the world. We are of relationship rather than in relationship.

The *state* of relationship is a *necessary* condition for being human.[9] From an existential perspective, we are Beings-in-the-world,[10] where an understanding of *being* cannot be found without an understanding of *world*.[11] We are inter-dependent creatures who cannot fall out of an inter-connected universe. On the contrary, if our skin-encapsulated egos will let us, our task is to fall deeper into contact with it. This interconnected being is what the free thinker Ervin Laszlo refers to in *Science and the Akashic Field*, as our state of entanglement.[12]

According to Laszlo and others we live in an 'in-formed' universe that is *meaningful in potential* from beneath the quantum level, suggesting that in our interactions with clients, the meaning that we make together cannot be attributed solely to the islands of client or therapist, or to a meaning-making function of the mind or brain. A human mind only is in so far she is entangled with at least one other, and we all have the capacity for transmission and reception at any given moment. Meaning or significance unfolds between us. According to Laszlo's field view, the space within and between is held as *meaningful in potential*. In the space between the two, a third can constellate.

The future beckons...

Near the start of my training I had a visit from a mercurial figure...

A dream... I am in a winter garden. The colours are shades of pale blues and silvers. At the centre of the garden there is a circular stone structure that holds a fountain of silvery iridescent water. Off to the right of the fountain there is a fig-

ure beckoning to me. He is a tall character wearing a hat, like a jester or a trickster, and I sense his mischief. Yet I also sense that he has something of significance to show me. He is dressed in a dandy suit of the palest, shimmering blue. As he calls me on, I notice he is showing me the frozen waste-lands that surround this wintery garden. In the snow I see a track of footsteps. He leads me on. I follow. He calls to me with a sense of purpose.

If we are more than the sum of our past and the recognition of our present context, then there is something about *where we are headed* or what calls to us from the future. In *The Soul's Code*, Hillman draws from Plato's 'Myth of Er' that tells how we each come into the world with a destiny or a paradeigma.[13] In Hillman, the idea that there is an individual image which belongs to each soul, is called 'the acorn theory'. It poetically describes how, at conception, we are endowed with a portion of fate, *Moira*, via our *daimon*.[14]

We can think of our daimon poetically, spiritually, or even bi-ologically if we wish, but either way, we are our daimon's carrier and it guides us with our unique interest at heart, according to our portion of fate. Hillman emphasizes that the daimon is not part of a fatalistic determinism. Our individual image does not predetermine our destiny. Instead, he urges us to treat our deci-sions and actions purposively, as though they matter because they matter for the daimon. And instead of looking to childhood and childhood experiences as being the cause of our current state, we will, in time, be able to read life backwards and see that, the *then* was for the sake of the *now*.

Aristotle named this way of looking at our actions and events, *telos*, or future cause. Hillman differentiates telos from teleology, preferring the original *telos*. Telos gives value to action, and gives events significance. It means that whatever happens is for the sake of something. With telos in the frame, it makes sense to read life backwards. Starting from the adult I am now, and reading back over the course of my life, what I am now doing makes sense ac-cording to the pattern of my daimon. From the standpoint of Psyche, moments infused with telos feel like the work of the Fates, those daughters of the Greek goddess Ananke (Necessity) who spin their threads, weaving the tapestry of experience and pulling our daimon close to us at our time of conception.

Growing down

> I said to my soul, be still and wait without hope, for hope would be hope for the wrong thing; wait without love, for love would be love of the wrong thing; there is yet faith, but the faith and the love are all in the waiting. Wait without thought, for you are not ready for thought: So the darkness shall be the light, and the stillness the dancing.[15]

In an anti-fatalist way, a soul-centred approach encourages us not to be attached to a particular outcome, but instead to grow down and wait – wait for the daimon to make itself known.

Growing down requires descending into chaotic messy or frozen depths. It involves a soulful spiralling pathway, rather than a linear spiritual ascent of onward and upward to a grand finale. Instead of growth or so-called progress, Re-Vision prefers the language of sustainability. This reflects an appreciation of the views of deep ecology: by descending into our deep bodies, we may uncover a deep sanity. Working with integrity requires staying with what we have – trusting our dream images, hearing our daimon. We spiral deeper into who we already are, trusting that this offers a new form of expansion and a wealth of potential treasure.

Through differing forms of reflective and creative exercises, students learn to attend to their life-world: their inner-world, inner constructs, emotional patterns of engagement, void spaces, fault lines, familial modes of connection and disconnection. A developmental understanding is vital in this process. The training aims to broaden and deepen the relational connection to self-other-world, so that the connection *feels* relational because there is deeper intrapersonal and interpersonal contact, and is held within a broader context. Students come to understand where the gaps from their unmet needs will have left fault lines in their inner worlds that will impact on their capacities as a trainee therapist. A personal fragment...

> *The dream of the Jung-like figure in Africa has another level of meaning for me, other than a reconnection to the impact of my grandfather's suicide. This alternate meaning is about the rupture that sought to tear apart my father's family. This was a dark star that pervaded my life in an unspoken drama. My uncle married an African woman and set his life up there. This seemed to exaggerate a rift in the relations with my father. However, two years before my uncle died tragically in a car crash, the brothers reconnected when my father went to visit him in Kenya. This reconciliation expanded my father's horizon, enabling to have the courage to create his brother's tomb when he died, and to participate in an African burial rite of passage for him in the Kenyan lands that had seemed to take him away.*

True relational engagement involves the dark as well as the light. It comes with tussle, jealousy, anger and mistrust. The groove is in the grit. Relationship is as much about *severance* and distance as it is about connection and contact. Severance and distance imply differentiation and is a dialectical step in the movement towards, or into, another psychological state. Re-Vision acknowledges the inevitability of darker forces at play in authentic relationships, recognizing the energy they hold. Interpersonal groups, and self and peer assessment sessions, offer spaces to practice giving and receiving challenges as well as encouragement and affirmation. These spaces offer the chance to sit with feelings of deep discomfort, as part of a preparation for working with clients.

Integration is not a once and for all process, we return again and again to our core struggles, making deeper sense of them through understanding and compassion, and earning, thereby, a sense of security.

Re-Vision Wheel Model

Whilst soul slips in through the keyhole, our minds need structure; we need rooms with walls that act as boundaries, doors that are points of entry and exit which can act as thresholds to the liminal realms. Re-Vision has a model and map to help ground and structure experience, remembering that whilst the map is not the territory, 'it sure helps us to get around'.[16]

The integrative transpersonal model that is held at Re-Vision is non-linear and pluralistic. It can be imagined as a tri-partite image. The journey around it is like tracking a pathway through a densely packed forest: spiralling inwards to a clear-lit space at the centre, a momentary taking stock of the gently filtered light, and then a tracking outwards again towards the periphery. This movement, encapsulated in the Wheel Model, has its roots in ideas of individuation, initiation and storytelling.

Timeless stories and myths become templates for individuation as we encounter the soul's journey. One such story is that of Psyche and Eros. Using the story of their relationship as a guiding myth, we witness Psyche's fall from grace as she holds up the lamplight whilst Eros sleeps.[17] Breaking her promise not to look, doubt overcomes her; she can't resist and so betrays Eros, which initiates a painful separation (psychological birth) and exile from him (her pre-ego attachment). She is cast out by Aphrodite to complete a number of difficult trials. We could call these the ego ordeals, which, from a developmental perspective, allow us to begin to differentiate and form an adult identity. Inevitably, this requires descending to the shadowy realms of underworld experience, as we face our limitations. This is the journey of the trials and tribulations of the therapeutic work: having taken a first glimpse behind a veil or mask of our adapted selves, we tumble, like Alice, down the rabbit hole into our less conscious, more unformed, shadowy selves. A trans-ego reunion occurs when the god Eros eventually relents and comes back to rescue Psyche in her hour of complete vulnerability (psychological death). The wheel gives a holding structure for this exile, descent and return, and helps us to make sense of individuation/developmental processes. It is, in one sense, the structure for the training.

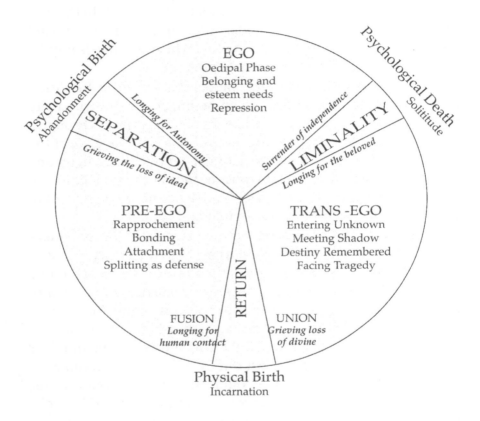

Figure 7.1. The Re-Vision Wheel, the cycle of initiation.

In many stories or myths there are three challenges, trials, or points of initiation. Re-Vision's Wheel Model also has three parts: i) pre-ego, ii) ego, iii) trans-ego.[18] These are delineated by three thresholds, which are liminal spaces where emotional development can make a quantum leap into another orbit or level of functioning. Thresholds mark transitions, where experiences of liminality invite us to connect with darker states such as grief (personal, cultural and ancestral). When we open ourselves to deep grief, we invite the possibility of a reawakening, and by surrendering we can experience moments of trans-ego interconnectivity. Yet, in the liminality of the threshold space, betwixt and between, we can feel lost. If we can wait with patience (which is not the same as hope), trusting and listening to Psyche's whispers, then a new perspective may offer itself up.

In 1909, Arnold Van Gennep introduced liminality to the field of anthropology in his seminal work, *Les rites de passage*.[19] Van Gennep described rites of passage, such as coming-of-age rituals and marriage, as having a three-part structure: separation, liminality and reassimilation. In the second part of the twentieth century, Victor Turner borrowed and expanded upon Van Gennep's concept of liminality, and its usage then spread to the therapeutic field.[20] Our Wheel Model has included and adapted Van Gennep's threshold markers, naming them separation, liminality and return. During training, the student, like an initiate, is required to undo some of their previous understanding to make way for the liminal period of their own learning transition. And finally, after their trials and work of deepening their individuation, they are endowed with a new status and returned to society, as counsellor or psychotherapist. This training process offers a grounding and mirroring model for holding uncertainty and the potential for change with our clients.

Threshold Madness

Turner offers a definition of liminality:

> Liminality may perhaps be regarded as the Nay to all positive structural assertions, but is in some sense the source of them all, and, more than that, as a realm of pure possibility whence novel configurations of ideas and relations may arise.[21]

Liminal states can bring high degrees of anxiety because they are essentially unknowable and uncontrollable; they are the 'nay' space. Liminal experiences can open up dysregulated or inchoate emotional states. If the tension inherent to this is held with a co-regulating other, a third place can emerge. In such states, our sense of the familiar is frustrated and there is an invitation to let go. It is this very vulnerability that makes thresholds so potentially creative and transformative, which is why they have always been used in rites of passage and initiation rituals. They hold the possibility of danger, death and nothingness as well creative transformation.

The Re-Vision Wheel Model, with ideas drawn from systems theorist Gregory Bateson, is visualized as a non-linear map: a spiralling pathway into the less conscious and hence less integrated aspects of our experience.[22] Such aspects are often detected via a subtle resonance and attunement with the field of our soulfully relational experience. The Wheel Model is a tool for navigating in the dark lands, imaginally offering our students a kind of holding as they are given the space within which they can slip.

Holding theory lightly can help us to make sense of our experience by 'reading life backwards'.[23] Models can creatively and playfully bridge differing perspectives, inviting coherence. In our model, we include Psyche's mythopoetic longing: her dreams, images, poems and intuitive divinations. And sometimes for change to occur, we re-frame from one perspective to another. Re-framing as a bridging activity helps to shift perspectives, allowing us to view the world through a different lens.

Ensouling field

How do you know but ev'ry Bird that cuts the airy way, is an immense World of Delight, clos'd by your senses five?[24]

One recurring epistemological problem in the field of psychotherapy relates to transference and countertransference phenomena, and to how we can know whose experience belongs to whom. We reframe this dualistic problem by accepting that we cannot know definitively, but we *can* attune with field constellations as a way of being-with liminality, and as a method for making sense of what emerges in the spaces between words.

The new relational paradigm in the social sciences and in anthropological studies included the shift to recognize that, in scientific method, the observer is always a participant and so the movement beyond Cartesian dualism (which splits mind from

MADNESS IN THE METHOD

body and soul from world) began. The new paradigm recognizes that we are embedded in our experience and can never truly be an objective observer. To make sense of our experience, we can reframe bipolar counter-transference and transference dynamics, using field terminology. In a greater interconnected context, the field can be imagined as a cosmic soul – a vast field of relationship or a reservoir of potentiality, like the wonderful image of Indra's net,[25] a metaphor used to illustrate the concepts of Śūnyatā (emptiness), pratītyasamutpāda (dependent origination), and interpenetration in Buddhist philosophy.[26] Holding the view that we are always engaged or entangled in the therapeutic field with our clients, offers a relationally soulful perspective, a radical intersubjectivity that resonates with contemporary approaches as well as ancient ones.

Field as Third

All real living is meeting.[27]

Field terminology is interdisciplinary – found in scientific, esoteric and therapeutic theories that relate to the fundamental nature of things and point to emergent processes. In both scientific and esoteric thinking, we find concepts of quantum fields, gravitational fields, morphogenic fields, and the Akashic field.[28] In psychotherapy texts, we read the terms intersubjective field,[29] interactive field,[30] and synergetic field. The shift from dualistic terminology reflects an increasing technological and systems-based application of the sciences on the one hand, and a shift into holistic practices on the other. Ideas from systems and process-based approaches include non-local causality, a-temporality and non-linear processing. Holding the concept of a *synergetic* field, we attempt to circumnavigate the epistemological question that arises in the consulting space. How can we know whose experience is whose? *Is this transference or counter-transference? Yours? Mine?* To be preoccupied with these questions would be to take the attention away from the therapeutic relationship and our presence in it. In practice, we experience a constellation of 'field as third' that we can surrender, attune, and attend to.

Including 'field as third' in our relational method brings its own rewards in a creative and potentially less shaming manner, than when working with 'two person' dynamics.[31] It's true that there are times (e.g., in an early alliance or pre-alliance phase of the work) when working within an analytic frame makes sense, and is perhaps more containing, but later on, when an alliance has been established and tested, a different way of being and knowing needs to be engaged with. We can then call upon our capacity for intuitive understanding, or *knowing through being*. We can meet one another in this space between, where our wounds intersect, creating something sublime. If we let go of our need to interpret, to always know, or logically make sense of what is going on in the spaces between us, and allow instead a trust in the wisdom of our deep body and the holding of a deeper context, then we can say with accuracy, 'It's all in the field'. Making sense comes later.

> *I'm sitting with a client – a young person with whom I've been working for two years and I'm thinking about how to let them know that unfortunately the service is closing down. It's a premature end and we'll have three months to 'work it through' but nevertheless there is a huge potential for a recapitulation of abandonment here, and I sense this. It's as though I'm sitting at the edge of a black hole that may pull me in. As I sit with discomfort and a sense of sadness, I notice a thought of wanting to give them something: a keepsake or symbol of our work together. I am holding this thought and wondering about it and what it means in the context of our work and our imminent end (am I wanting to rescue or somehow assuage my guilt for leaving?). My thoughts fleetingly turn to a close friend of mine who wears a name on a necklace that helps her to hold a certain person in mind. Then I'm back to the room and my client asks me if I'll return after the break. We then go on to talk about how I won't be back. During what is then a very difficult discussion, they ask if they can keep my name badge which I wear around my neck! We had attuned in the darkness. I did leave three months later and they did not take my name*

badge. But every time I see it in my drawer at home, I think of them and wonder how they are. Somehow our worlds remain entangled.

Field as Abyss

He who fights with monsters might take care lest he thereby become a monster. And when you gaze long into the abyss, the abyss also gazes into you.[32]

Working with the field can at times feel maddening, like sitting on the edge of an abyss which is seemingly unknowable to its core. This feels like the 'dark third'. Facing into this abyss brings us into contact with a dreadful sense that here anything could happen, and our mind then scrambles to know. In the quote above, Nietzsche reminds us that, when we encounter the field as abyss, the abyss has us, as much as we have it. Sitting with risk, we feel the danger of being consumed, swallowed alive. Yet staring into the abyss can have a deeply creative potential.

A composite case vignette:

> *Client X has a history of extreme trauma and neglect; his life experiences have fragmented his sense of being. He has many parts and each has a different story to tell. Before I realized the extent of his shattered being, I experienced sessions with long, deeply dissociated states. It was as if he would leave the space and I felt myself at times either being pulled into another dimension with him or feeling a million miles away. These spaces felt at times maddening, like facing into a dark, bottomless pit. With his psychiatric diagnosis of borderline personality disorder, I was advised to provide clear and consistent boundaries. Keep everything in the session and stick to the contract! And yet as I allowed myself over time, over years, to be guided by his own states and follow him into his dissociation, and experience the fragmentation and despair characterized by an unknowing, the so-called borderline phenomena dissolved as hidden characters came into contact with me. It was as though we had*

to encounter the liminality together in order to give a place for all the half-formed or chaotic fragments to present themselves. We then embarked on a journey of re-contracting the boundaries with each alter ego, as they each required to be treated as unique beings.

Staring into an abyss, we face into the dark side of nature, experience, or behaviour. There can be deeply uncomfortable silences that evoke the rescuer, or long saturnine moods that hover over or within us. Or a black hole-like energy can come, which consumes all that falls near it. There can be moments of fragmentation or dissociation, where the other may momentarily disappear from contact. Like a dark star in the heart, we find aspects of our attitudes and behaviours that we would rather bracket off, or project with dualistic thinking. The abyss can be seen narrowly, as the Jungian shadow archetype, or, more broadly and existentially, as facing into our denial, self-betrayal, mortality, trauma, emotional futility and grief. As such, we face into our human limitations. A soul-centred approach encourages students to give darkness a place, to allow themselves to disturb and be disturbed, allowing the abyss to be present and creative in the work. And this requires us to allow a certain amount of chaos over the threshold. This is tough, as our rational minds will pull at us to structure our experience into either/or thinking: diagnosing and pathologizing ourselves (as with the voice of the inner critic), and our clients (by trying to find out what is 'wrong' with them).

We need a robust capacity to hold what is in the field, to allow this disturbance to be present and still pay homage to the power of the energies of the abyss and not be pulled in and overwhelmed. For this we require ethical boundaries, understanding of trauma, good supervision and a willingness to be reflective. Also, we require an approach that holds the authentic relationship between client and therapist as being central to the process of change. Perhaps such authenticity necessitates a little madness, or a little reframing of madness as a movement towards a deeper wisdom – a wild wisdom.

In one telling, the primordial God Chaos gives birth to Eros. So it falls on us to stay with the unformed darkness, energetically giving Chaos a place. As trainers and therapists, we are required to give disorder its rightful space: to carry Chaos, to accept that it belongs, and to realize that suffering in the therapy process is for something – in order to give birth to Eros. At first, Psyche's glance led to her imagining Eros to be a monster; a moment of madness saw her betray the trust of her lover, which took her on a path of the dark night of the soul. Without this moment and the ensuing loss, transformation may not have occurred. When she betrayed him, Eros turned his back on her, yet this act of abandonment ultimately led to her reclaiming herself. A tough kind of severing love eventually brought Psyche home to Eros, a reunion which gave birth to Joy.

With Eros imagined as an archetype of the resonant field, we weave a connection of a deep, authentic, trusting and loving alliance with the client, but one that is not without trials and that can withstand doubt and experiences of rupture or betrayal. From a psycho-neurobiological level, we can talk about Eros as a right hemispheric (person to person) resonance: one that encourages 'threshold moments' to become creative and expansive experiences that can usher in the potential of structural change. From a more humanistic perspective, we could imagine Eros as instigating dialogical, or I-Thou moments of meeting, that can reveal who we are to the other and to ourselves. And speaking trans-personally, we can feel Eros in moments of deeply felt interconnectivity with all beings.

The Return

A dream fragment from forty-two years ago...

There's a soft knocking at my window, I feel curious and frightened. I gently peel back the curtain and there, on the other side of the pane of glass, is a wolf standing up and staring at me, with his yellow eyes glowing in the dark.

Inevitably, we return from moments of divine madness, perhaps with a windswept feeling. Yet Hillman reminds us that when we welcome the wild ones in, they become a little more domesticated, so it's a good idea to leave a bowl of milk on the threshold. Spiralling back in to the bread and butter of the work, we return from moments of deep felt interconnectivity, back to the humdrum, the more usual rhythm of everyday relationship. If Psyche has been honoured we might bring something back with us, perhaps a soothing balm or ointment. Nevertheless, we will, sooner or later, again find ourselves in the fractured ground of our pre-ego struggles. Neurotic anxieties will present in the field. New seeds will be buried again and will begin to root in more fertile earth, having been primed with the bloom, fruit and decay of previous rounds.

For students, after the initial excitement and passion of opening to something new with a client, essays and case studies still have to be written. For clients, there will still be disillusioning or pragmatic transactions: fees have to be paid, they will feel let down in a mis-attuned moment. Therapists return to the familial fold, to the washing up and school runs. After the bliss, the laundry. Life goes on.

On reflection, I can see that there is much that is unsaid in this chapter, and probably something that is said too much. I can feel a tension between connection and severance throughout. Writing this, I have felt both excited by it and lost with it, so the process reflects the content. However, what *is* said here emerges from my own experience and my own passion for an approach that continues to welcome me home.

[1] Karl Kerenyi and James Hillman, *Oedipal Variations: Studies in Literature and Psychoanalysis* (Woodstock, CT: Spring Publications, 1991), p. 98.

[2] David Bohm, *Wholeness and the Implicate Order* (London and New York: Routledge, 1995).

[3] Kerenyi and Hillman, *Oedipal Variations*, p. 98.

[4] James Hillman, *Revisioning Psychology* (New York: Harper Perennial, 1998), p. 71.

[5] Hillman, *Revisioning Psychology*, p. 57.

[6] Coleman Barks, *Rumi: Selected Poems* (London: Penguin Books Ltd, 1999), p. 36.

[7] The concept was first laid out in the Emerald Tablet of Hermes Trismegistus: 'That which is Below corresponds to that which is Above, and that which is Above, corresponds to that which is Below, to accomplish the miracles of the One Thing'.

[8] Donald Winnicott, 'Further thoughts on babies as persons', in J. Hardenberg, ed., *The Child and the Outside World: Studies in developing relationships* (London: Tavistock Publications Ltd., 1957), p. 137.

[9] Daniel Stern, *The Interpersonal World of the Infant* (London and New York: Routledge, Taylor Francis Group, 2018).

[10] Martin Heidegger, *Being and Time* (Oxford and Cambridge, MA: Blackwell Publishing Ltd, 1962).

[11] Robert Stolorow and George Atwood, *Contexts of Being: The Intersubjective Foundations of Psychological Life* (New York and Oxford: Routledge, Taylor and Francis Group, 2002).

[12] James Hillman, *The Soul's Code: In Search of Character and Calling* (London, New York, Toronto, Sydney and Auckland: Bantam Books, 1996).

[13] Hillman, *The Soul's Code*.

[14] This is Hillman's spelling of the Latin *daemon*.

[15] D. H. Lawrence, *The Complete Poems of D.H. Lawrence* (New York: Viking Press, 1971).

[16] Peter Levine, *In an Unspoken Voice: How the Body Releases Trauma and Restores Goodness* (Berkeley, CA: North Atlantic Books, 2010).

[17] Chris Robertson and Dawn Freshwater, *Emotions and Needs: Core Concepts in Therapy* (Buckingham and New York: Open University Press, 2002).

[18] Robertson and Freshwater, *Emotions and Needs*.

[19] Arnold Van Gennep, *The Rites of Passage: Anthropology and Ethnography* (London and Henley: Routledge and Kegan Paul, 1960).

[20] Victor Turner, *The Forest of Symbols: Aspects of Ndembu ritual* (New York: Cornell University Press, 1967).

[21] Turner, *The Forest of Symbols*, p. 97.

[22] Gregory Bateson, *Steps to an Ecology of Mind* (Chicago, IL, and London: The University of Chicago Press, 1972).

[23] Dick Russell, *The Life and Ideas of James Hillman, Vol 1: The Making of a Psychologist* (New York: Helios Press, 2013).

[24] William Blake, *The Marriage of Heaven and Hell: Illuminated Manuscript with Original Illustrations by William Blake.* (Oxford: Oxford University Press, 1975)

[25] Victor Sogen Hori, Richard P. Hayes, and James Mark Shields, *Teaching Buddhism in the West; from the Wheel to the Web* (London: RoutledgeCurzon, 2002).

[26] 'Indra's Net', Wikipedia, at https://en.wikipedia.org/wiki/Indra%27s_net (accessed 17 July 2018).

[27] Martin Buber, cited in Richard Hycner, *Between Person and Person: Toward a Dialogical Psychotherapy* (Highland, NY: The Gestalt Journal Press, 1993).

[28] Rupert Sheldrake website, at https://www.sheldrake.org (accessed 17 July 2018).

[29] Robert D. Stolorow and George E. Atwood, *Contexts of Being: The Intersubjective Foundations of Psychological Life* (New York, NY, and Oxford: Routledge, Taylor and Francis Group, 2002).

[30] Murray Stein, ed., *The Interactive Field in Analysis* (Wilmette, IL: Chiron Publications, 1995).

[31] As described in Richard Hycner, *Between Person and Person: Toward a Dialogical Psychotherapy* (Highland, NY: The Gestalt Journal Press, 1993).

[32] Friedrich Nietzsche, *Beyond Good and Evil* (New York: Vintage Books, 1989), p. 146.

Chapter 8

Maps for Soul Making:
Story Enactment in Psychotherapy
Mary Smail

'It's something about...'

This is a phrase which is repeatedly used when people find a new aspect of themselves through the hearing or enactment of a story. It is used when a place or quality arises out of the wisdom of implicit imaginal knowing which is not yet sufficiently formed to emerge into consciousness and communication. The phrase is consistently used when Narnia is discovered at the back of the wardrobe and suddenly Aslan's presence meets you where you have been frozen. It is used when the Greek myth of Odysseus and his epic sea voyage offers a framework for a personal struggle with lostness and an inability to find your way home. The impact of this is hard to explain and tricky to understand. An imaginative encounter has ordered a shift in the internal world which cannot be articulated immediately externally. A person in this process, trying to convey it to another, will frequently look downwards; they will be stuck for words and avoid eye contact as they falteringly try to describe an important revelation, an 'aha' moment. At this point, three words are often used, 'It's something about. It's something about ...'. These words are a promise of something that is not yet definite preparing to make the transition from imaginative intelligence into everyday life.

The phrase, 'It's something about...', appears to flag up a crossover places where an image, recognized internally but which cannot be consciously stated, attempts an opening articulation. An unmet element of the depths makes a first annunciation, offering more than has previously been available. It is a way of struggling to construct what is recognized inside, but is not able to be consciously defined. 'It's something about...' has a story feel to it; it is like finding a piece of a jigsaw puzzle, liking the colour, but not knowing where to place it as the full picture is not yet fully clear.

This chapter will have an It's-Something-About quality as it explores how soul stories bring symbolic image fragments into consciousness to emerge as the first fruits in a transformation process. It will look at how traditional story can provide soul maps, at soul making, and at the possibility of a secular spirituality emerging when soul is released from theological capture. It will 'stand on the shoulders of giants' to consider how the work of James Hillman's archetypal psychology, which promotes image and leans on story, is amplified by the addition of embodied enactment. It will try to convey how the cycle of soul stories and the moving body both enable deeply embodied ways of learning in Re-Vision's psychotherapy training. And, of course, this chapter will contain several stories.

Soul: religious or secular?

What it was that Earth-Maker-Great-Spirit created at the beginning of consciousness, we will never know. What we do know is that Earth-Maker moved a right arm and then a left arm and moved as he thought about what needed to happen. Tears began to flow and fall, and slowly they formed into waters. In this way, Earth-Maker realized! Movement became thinking, and what was wished for came into existence. In this way, Earth-Maker wished for light, and then the earth, and so they all became.

Then, Earth-Maker wished for company. Picking up soil, Earth-Maker formed a Being which was well made, but which had no mind to think. So, Earth-Maker made a mind and spoke to Being, but there was no answer. So, Earth-Maker made Being a tongue, but still no reply. Then Earth-Maker realized. Being had no soul. So, Earth-Maker made Being a soul and listened as Being tried to say something which was very unclear. So, Earth-Maker breathed. Earth-Maker breathed into Being. And then, at last they spoke.[1]

There are many Creation Myths, like the Native American story above, which talk about an essence of the creator being placed in the created and in that sharing they become one. The story holds no apology for there being a 'creator' space within humankind, and variations on this theme are repeated in the myths of all world cultures. It is there in the Sioux story of the Creator hiding within his creation until they are ready to find him. It is there in the Hasidic tale where God is said to whisper all the secrets of the universe to us only for us to forget as soon as we are born. And it can be found in the ninth century BC story where The One divides and becomes The Two and so is present in everything. Such stories carry a trace from a time when it was known that humanity and divinity are inherently and vitally connected and belong to each other.

The simplicity of what Story can offer us about numinous companionship often becomes imprisoned when it becomes established in religious teaching. From the Christian point of view, the evangelical branches of the church regard the soul as the vessel for the eternal aspect of the human who, left to her own devices, falls into sin or sickness. Repentance saves the soul and she is cherished in her redeemed state, so long as she keeps pure. It is all conditional and does not make space for shadow. The creation story, however, tells of Earth-Maker's need to invest Being with a soul, so that creator and created can be in relationship. There is no Credo or dogma here, nor any debate on how to set the terms. The story simply promotes an unconditional notion of humanity and the 'Goddish' – call it Love or Grace if the 'God' word has become tainted – sharing breath with each other. Without need for holy scripture or religious language, the story notion offers the essence of theology, but without the vestments of religious doctrine. Human beings and Great Spirit-Earth Maker need the company of each other and are bound by breath. It's a kind of secular spirituality, released out of creed and held in the folklore, in which there is space for all.

James Hillman speaks of the relationship between the Christian church and the soul in mythology in story. He says,

> I try to bypass the Christian view by stepping behind it to the Greeks, to polytheism... The big job is to free the psychological material from those Christian meanings. One way to do this might be to show that these Christian meanings exist outside of the Christian approach, outside of the dogma that already says what they mean.[2]

He goes on to say he wants to free the mythical basis of the soul from Christian interpretation. Soul making needs a wider story to offer a window into what lies deep within each person. It needs an inclusive and soft knowing, an 'under-standing' which comes from the individual freedom to find Earth-Maker uniquely, where there is space to breathe together.

Metaphor in story as soul language

Although a soul experience may be strong and alive inside, it needs to be slow to find a way back to words and to be shared with others in a verbal form. The soul rarely speaks to us in thesis but uses experience and metaphor as its way of bringing change. Joseph Campbell talks about these wordless epiphanies as 'the best things'. He says they cannot be told because they are beyond thought.

> The best things can't be told because they transcend thought.
> The second best are understood, because they are thoughts that are supposed to refer to that which can't be thought about.
> The third best are what we talk about.
> And myth is that field of reference to what is absolutely transcendent.[3]

A story is a series of metaphors which bring something that is not yet known closer into reach through the imagination. Stories are epistemological in nature because they affect and involve both the storyteller and hearer by bringing new insight. They provide dramatic distance by slipping around resistance or defences and finding a way inside. Working through a story offers a container and place for both client and therapist to meet indirectly, where the external world with its quandaries disappears for a time, and a creative storyland is visited. Here client and therapist can discover what is waiting to be found. Finding a myth or fairy tale that resonates with my life story, feeling that someone has been through this before, provides sustenance and dissolves the isolation of pathology and distress. There is room for a healthy re-seeing which comes back to the everyday through metaphor.

Metaphors, because they are multi-faceted and multi-layered, act as windows which allow us to look through and meet the untellable 'best things which transcend thought' that Campbell describes. In a therapeutic context, images described through metaphor provide therapist and client a means to look together and see different aspects of what is emerging from the inner story, without tying it down by applying it over-quickly to everyday life. These images need time to be experienced before a meaning harvest can be gathered. If explanation comes in too quickly, the potency of what is found imaginatively is compromised through intellectual explanation, and the mystery of what is symbolic, powerful and transformational is diluted and dispelled.

James Hillman writes about this,

> If we are ill ... we get well because of the imagination... Therapy is one way to revive the imagination and exercise it. The entire therapeutic business is this sort of imaginative exercise. It picks up the oral tradition of telling stories, therapy re-stories life... Therapy has to be so concerned with the childish part of us in order to recreate and exercise the imagination.[4]

A client coming to therapy brings a story of everyday life which is narrated to the therapist, often from a place of limitation or distress. In telling and sharing this narrative story, the presenting difficulty comes into relationship with another person and is no longer hidden and solitary. We hear again from James Hillman in his book *Healing Fiction* where he speaks poignantly of this process,

> In each case, the story leads into therapy... And this also means that I the therapist-writer have now entered the

tale, in fact, become a key figure in the story whose beginnings, development, plot, and style have had until this
meeting, nothing to do with me...

Yet there was no story in the therapeutic genre until 'I'
got into it, so that from the moment the person crosses
the threshold into therapy a whole new story begins...[5]

There is yet more on offer when we move into mythology.
When a myth is introduced in therapy, the narrative story, with
all its idiosyncratic twists and turns, is met by an ancient story
which has been passed through the oral tradition of storytelling
for thousands of years and kept alive because it holds a map for
living. These old myths and tales shift consciousness from outside
concerns and move the hearer inwards, to the unconscious place
of the archetypes: the primordial images and patterns which structure our emotional experience. Carl Jung speaks of these
archetypes as being 'the most powerful ideas in history'.[6] They are
images and motivations that come from the earliest experience of
human beings that teach us how to live both our individual and
collective life beyond an external need for approval. Through the
shape and characters of a story, archetypal energy can be playfully
explored so that what is found in the character's journey can become a resource for our own. Stories are the containers for
archetypal maps, translating slowly back to the here and now,
through metaphor.

Thomas Moore states,

> Story is an excellent way of caring for the soul. It helps
> us see the themes that circle in our lives, the deep
> themes that tell the myths we live. It would take only a
> slight shift in emphasis in therapy to focus on the story-
> telling itself rather than on its interpretation.[7]

Risha, 24-year-old with a history of self-harm bears this theory out,

> I was really stuck and I felt cutting myself was the only
> way I could communicate how hopeless I felt inside.
> When I heard the fairy tale of *The Three Feathers*, I didn't
> feel like Simple, I *was* him. Like him, I am alone in the

world, but my other world was full of wonderful things which I could not see until I had opened the trapdoor underneath me and made my way down. I don't know where this is going in my life, but that story gave me hope that I don't have to try so hard.[8]

The story with its beginning, middle and end series of symbols provides a metaphoric language and a map to a new perspective in the psychotherapy process.

Soul story in the therapy room

People come to counselling or therapy because they are searching. Something in their life is blocking their spontaneity and freedom to live life well. Somewhere along their way, they have tangled with some form of death-in-life, had an interruption to health, or the breakdown of relationship. Fear of not making it, or a sense of being different, is making them feel 'less than'. To work soulfully, the therapist needs to be able to create a place where imagination and soul can be at home together. In my practice, I need to be able to say something about the invisible without prescribing 'how-to' methods. The stories help to do this.

Peter was a Doctor of psychology, working in a large medical hospital library researching Cognitive Behaviour Therapy with Borderline Personality Disorder patients.[9] He was young, earnest, and exhausted. He had contacted me because he was drawn by the SoulWorks name of my webpage. He told me that he didn't really get what it was talking about, but he had liked reading it. He said he wanted to find a different kind map for his life and to get to what know this soul stuff was about, though he was not sure everyone had one. After a few sessions, he wanted me to talk about why I placed an emphasis on soul. Instead of doing this, I began to tell him a story.

Once there was an old man, a hunter, who had lived long and full, but who knew that there was something he was looking for. One day he made his way down to the lake, close to his village and bending down to fill his calabash, he saw a reflection in the water. It was an enormous white bird. Astonished, he looked up, but the bird had vanished over the forest of the night, as if it had never been. From that moment on, the man was filled with restless longing to find and keep the bird.

Leaving his village and home and cattle, he travelled to the north, the south, the east and the west. While there were rumours of such a creature, no one knew where the bird was. All his life was spent searching till eventually he heard that it lived on the great mountain, very close to his home. Returning there, he climbed until he found himself at the top of the mountain, but there was no sign of the bird. Falling deep into despair he threw himself to the ground and wept. Then, something impelled him to look up, a voice perhaps? As he did, a single feather fell from the sky and into his lap and in that moment, he knew.

What sort of bird was it? This story teller cannot say, its name was never spoken. What can be said though, is that it was a great white bird and one feather in the hand of a human is enough. A feather is a good place for longing to find a way and follow.[10]

Although I have my own thoughts and ever-changing experience of what soulmaking is, conveying this to Peter was not really what was needed, though it did inform how I chose the story which I brought to him. 'The White Bird' offered Peter a metaphor for beginning a search and allowed him to talk about the old man's despair, separate from his own. He talked about the validity of longing as a road to finding, though he still wondered if there was a bird to find. He tentatively began to use the term 'feather-ness', which together we decided was something breezy that could pull him away from heaviness and loosen him up. He moved as he spoke of this feathery feeling, gesturing with his right hand raised and spiralling round his head.

The soul of the client is always waiting to find a way into the therapy. It is making invitations continually through half-said nuances, through gestures and through the feelings in the room.

Words are of course essential, but there is a need to journey into what cannot be spoken now and then, to retrieve what is waiting there and gradually return with it. To do so we have to tend to metaphoric thinking – the 'something about' which comes before understanding. The therapist has to be prepared to flail around and feel lumpy and awkward until together, therapist and client, find a thread and the work moves into a deeper place.

Peter's body brought the movement and I moved forward to meet it. What if body could be the non-verbal library or re-search department, for something he needed to know? What if the first utterances of soul talk could be born through a movement? I asked him to amplify the movement and to make more of it, as if it had something it wanted him to know, beyond what he and I could talk our way into. I suggested that, for a short time, he ask any dis-comfort or inner critic part to stand back. Just for a moment, could he trust the language of his body?

Later he said he worked with the movement because I seemed to know what I was doing and was at home with it. I did not feel at home. I knew what I was asking Peter to do was awkward for us both. The 'at homeness' he invested in me was a mirror for his own witnessing of an 'unvisited' part of himself, which he now felt taken seriously. The word 'feather-ness' offered itself to Peter. Where he had been so heady and stuck in the literal, he began to entertain the idea of there being another part of him which knew things differently. This satisfied Peter and gave a changed meaning to his work and latterly to his relationships, certainly with me, but more importantly with other people in the world outside therapy. Through entering the story imaginatively and doing more than thinking about it, a new map for life emerged. Peter began to live more lightly and although his outer situation had not changed, his soul-feather connection enabled him to feel he was accompa-nied. He no longer felt alone.

The Irish poet and philosopher John O'Donohue talks of this,

> The imagination retains a passion for freedom. There are no rules for the imagination. It never wants to stay trapped in the expected territories. The old maps never

satisfy it. It wants to press ahead beyond the accepted frontiers and bring back reports of regions no mapmaker has yet visited.[11]

Story maps, embodiment and re-visioning

What kind of education shall we give them then? We shall find it difficult to improve on the time honoured distinction between the physical training we give to the body and the education we give to the mind and character... And we shall begin by educating mind and character, shall we not? In this education you would include stories, would you not?[12]

In his book, *The Soul's Code*, James Hillman gives passing reference to the Greek Platonic story, 'The Myth of Er'. The book is based around this myth, but curiously the story is referenced in a few lines, dryly written, which Hillman calls 'a nutshell'.[13] He offers the story in its most minimal form and then draws out the theory and inspiration for his life-changing and highly successful book.

Some years ago, Hillman participated on a day called Invisible Values, where it was agreed that he would bring what he called 'a soul-take on the invisibles', but before he spoke, participants would have the chance to enact 'The Myth of Er' together. The day started with 63 people enacting the ancient story, while Hillman warily watched his nutshell seven-line story take on flesh. The story was told, not read, and then re-told by everyone present, using movement, gesture and non-verbal sound. There were minimal words. At the end, James Hillman was no longer cautious. He leaned over excitedly and said to me, 'This is amazing! This soul thing I write about, it is so real'.

It was an epiphany moment, a recognition and an agreement. Soul making needs more than just the head. Soul needs to be present through embodied imagination, the re-telling of stories, incarnated in community. Soul needs the ritual of applied enactment for something fresh and new to emerge. At Re-Vision, myths such as The Holy Grail, Pandora's Box and Chiron the Wounded Healer are back-bones which give people the chance to meet and process key archetypal themes. This working through of myths and stories holds a mirror to developmental thresholds and is an intrinsic feature of the training in the first year course which is called 'The Soul's Journey'. In the latter part of that year, students enact something of their own mythic stories in collaboration with peers. These enactments bring both personal issues and archetypal themes into intense living connection and draw out meaning.

Over the last four years, enactment of traditional story has been introduced to the psychotherapy training using a form for enactment called the Sesame Approach, which has six phases – a Focus, Warm Up, Bridge-In, Enactment, Bridge-out and Grounding – enabling body and imagination into a place where participants can be free of self-consciousness and are able to work spontaneously. This ritual form is flexible enough to allow participants to re-tell the story in their own way while being firm enough to contain and ground the process. The form makes it sufficiently safe for people to move beyond ego insecurity, so they can be open to the surprises of what emerges when their soul explores a story through the moving body.

Psychotherapy students are asked to take a risk by working in an embodied way. Initially, resistance comes up. 'I can't move – it terrifies me'. 'I won't be able to act'. 'Is this Am Dram?' On the contrary, working in this way is not about performing, talent, or ability. It is about unconscious processes having a chance to emerge through the distance and safety of a role, so that through the enactment of an archetypal character, new possibility emerges. It is one thing to discuss a story and link it to what you think it says about your own life, but there is added depth when a character who draws you in offers you a genuinely new way of seeing. Robert Romanyshyn sums this up in this way,

> Embodying psyche is the crucial path towards a radical ethics that closes the gap between psychological insight and becoming what we wish to know.[14]

Students are asked to learn through a cycle of stories, each of which has been chosen for its potential to offer an imaginary way of perceiving soul qualities through the beginning, middle and end of each story told. They are asked to hear the story, select a character, embody the character spontaneously, and reflect personally on the process through either movement, drawing or journaling. They are asked to make links to existing theory and consider how a particular story might deepen their therapeutic practice working with other people. It is up to each person to choose what they want to do, and although the telling of the story is facilitated and held, the enactments are free and open. Anything can happen and it does! The illustration below shows one possible selection of stories which might be used.

Figure 8.1. Cycle of stories wheel.[15]

- *Before the Beginning* stories look imaginatively at what might have been before we existed.

- *Arriving* stories talk about how it is to arrive on Earth.

- *Growing up* stories look at a character's becoming journey – the hurdles and trials of taking up a place here.

- *Soul Presence* stories look at the call of the soul and soul meaning.

- *Soul Values* stories tell of soul qualities – lostness, woundedness, not knowing, longing, surrender, grace.

- *Death* stories talk of meeting or running away from death, and what is happening for the soul at these times.

- *After the End* stories are about what is beyond an edge. What we can find if we begin to listen to hunches and intuitions about people we have lost, or about our own journey when it will be beyond where we are now.

Psychotherapy students who have been through this process have generously agreed for me to use excerpts from their end of module essays. The excerpts come under four common response categories when people are invited to embody soul:

- How do I get out of my head?

- I really do not want to do this.

- What is this for?

- How will this affect my therapy practice?

The excerpts now follow.

- *Getting out of the head*
  I am particularly aware (now) that my go-to place when stressed is my head – my rational mind. And this at the expense of attention to my feelings – as registered in my body. Through the enactment of story characters, the

Shaman in the Gopher American first nation story, the Father King of Inanna and others, I experienced the replacing of my own persona/mask with that of another and for a time became another. What is significant for me is that when re-donning my own everyday persona/mask I found that it fitted a little looser. What feels right is that there is less of me, so to speak, my self-consciousness, and more availability to take in the other to see them in their world and offer empathy.

- *Resistance*
During our training enactment Mary offered us invitations and alternative choices, I know that I couldn't see those choices for myself in character at the time. I could play with the suggestions and test out where my character could authentically move. Ironically Mary's acknowledgment that I didn't want to play enlarged the area of our mutual imaging by including my authentic responses. This allowed me to feel my anger, frustration, fear and frozenness and feel a sense of sharing, showing and being seen. I suggest these moments of seeming story/play failure are a call to reach down further to where the nourishment really is. This story enactment is a return to a way of working with my own process, and I was more than a little surprised to notice how much I have not been using these techniques. I had unconsciously sided with my client's resistance. My arrogance, or my agenda, shows up in a moment of, 'I know what you need from this story'. Of course, I don't! My not-knowing vulnerability can bring more depth of intimacy if I hang in there with my embarrassment.

- *Embodiment changing the dimension*
The impact on me has been to move me into a more four-dimensional experience of life. In their abridged form, the stories seem to me equivalent to the most pared down black line drawings. In this flat-on-the-page

aspect they are like a map depicting the territory. As soon as the group inhabited the characters, it was as if the flat word drawings on the page inflated and took up three-dimensional space in the room. In embodying a character, I felt that I was creating space for them internally – separate from, yet connected to, my life narrative of who I have experienced myself as being. It was the creation of this new space within me that gave me the sense of a fourth dimensional experience of life; a sense of greater inner differentiation, connecting me to a greater complexity beneath the surface which feels like soul-making. I noticed a change in the way I relate to others.

- *Implications for practice*
  And what of my own practice? In many respects I feel I am still processing my training experience. However, I have become more confident in asking clients, if they are willing, to expand a gesture that looks incomplete in order to explore what the movement wants to express. I have had a personal experience whilst role playing a client and looking through a collection of pebbles and shells at just how powerfully such a simple activity can fire the imagination and naturally allow the emergence of things that need to be spoken. Most importantly, I feel I have developed greater confidence in holding a wider symbolic perspective. Stories have supported me in holding the client in a deeper, yet more trusting, connection, or in understanding what my role is in our work together at that particular stage in the work.

I would like to end with a quote from Robert Romanyshyn, with whom I have had the opportunity to work on several occasions when soul has been allowed to move between thoughts and poetry to story and enactment and from there to fresh insights that can be spoken and shared. This work has been rich and free and fun. I believe soul needs fun. I asked him how he would sum up our work for this chapter, as what he and I have been evolving has played a part in The Stories of Soul Making course on the psychotherapy training at Re-Vision. He writes:

> When I was writing my book, *The Frankenstein Prophecies: Who is the Monster?* (now completed) Mary Smail had arranged with her group of therapists to enact the story and some of its themes. Much to my delight I realized the beautiful and powerful convergence between our approaches to soul making. As a phenomenological depth psychologist who had done much work with actors and had developed an approach to dream work that embodies the dream, I was all in favour of an approach about story making, imagination and embodiment. In this first work together through her students under her guidance, the Monster was there, a real living presence, a piece of soul magic. I realized that my approach had to be amplified and deepened. I knew that working together from converging perspectives we were developing an approach to soul work in which the matter of soul work is work in which soul matters, is on display, makes a scene, and gives flesh to dreams, stories and imagination.[16]

Ending thoughts

This chapter has looked at how Story allows the promptings and leadings of the human soul to link us to elements of mystery, which are akin to the traditional spiritual tenets of organized religion. It has considered how telling a story in therapy opens up an imaginative landscape which client and therapist can share, and how this process is amplified when embodiment of story and metaphoric language are made explicitly welcome in psychotherapeutic practice. It has described some of the qualities which are needed by the story-trusting therapist when they utilize the immense resource of world stories waiting to be found and used in a healing process.

I end this process with one last story, which comes from the first-generation people of America.

Once, a herdsman, who tended a herd of cows, found that the udders of his creatures were dry and there was not a drop of milk to drink. He wondered at this, for the grass was green and nourishing and he realized something was wrong. He hid by night to watch the herd.

As he watched, a rope fell from the sky and beautiful sky women descended, each carrying a basket. The sky women milked the cows and drank the milk, but when the man ran out to challenge them, they ran to the rope to escape. One of them was too slow to reach it, and after talking, it was agreed she would stay with the herdsman, on the condition that he would never look inside her basket. It was agreed and they lived well together, with her basket resting in a corner of their dwelling.

One day, when the sky woman was out, the man had an overwhelming urge to open the basket. Impulsively disregarding the condition, he opened the lid and what he saw made him laugh. Later when the sky woman returned, she immediately knew what he had done, and when she asked him, he said,

'You silly woman – there is nothing in the basket'.

'You saw nothing?' she said.

'No, it is empty,' he replied.

The sky woman lifted her basket and walked away from the dwelling. She never returned."[17]

Soul knowing, like the sky woman, will come down to Earth and guide us when certain conditions are in place. We need to develop soft eyes for nuances and hunches and not rush to pry off the lid of seemingly empty baskets and harm invisible realities. When we can do this, the rewards are profound. One way is to turn to the simplicity of stories with courage and let them do the work. They will lead us to find something more about soul and a pathway on to 'living happily ever after'.

1 Josepha Sherman, *Mythology for Storytellers* (London: Routledge, 2015), p. 76. Re-told for enactment by Mary Smail in 2013.

2 James Hillman. *Inter Views* (Dallas, TX: Spring Publications, 1983), pp. 75 – 76.

3 Joseph Campbell and Bill Moyers, *The Power of Myth* (London, New York: Doubleday, 1986), p. 46.

4 James Hillman, *Healing Fiction* (Dallas, TX: Spring Publications, 1983), p. 47.

5 Hillman, *Healing Fiction*, p.16.

6 Carl Jung, *The Structure and Dynamics of the Psyche* (London: Routledge, 1960), CW 8 para 342.s

7 Thomas Moore, *Care of the Soul* (New York: Harper Perennial, 1994), p. 13.

8 Risha's details have been deliberately changed to preserve anonymity, but the events depicted took place.

9 Peter's details have been deliberately changed to preserve anonymity, but the events depicted took place.

10 Laurens Van der Post, *The Heart of the Hunter* (UK: Vintage Classics, 1968), p. 167. Re-told for enactment by Mary Smail in 2008.

11 John O'Donohue, *Beauty* (London: Harper Collins, 2004), p.145.

12 Plato, *The Republic*, trans. Desmond Lee, Part 3 (https://erenow.com/ancient/the-republic/5.html).

13 James Hillman, *The Soul's Code* (Great Britain: Bantam, 1996), p. 8.

14 Robert Romanyshyn in an email to Mary Smail, February 2017.

15 Story Cycle diagram with thanks to Jo Van den Broek.

16 Robert Romanyshyn, written for this chapter, May 2018.

17 'The Sky Woman's Basket', African folk tale. Source unknown.

Chapter 9

Knowing of a Third Kind
Chris Robertson

This chapter attempts to set out some of the underpinnings to the integrative training at Re-Vision. It does not pretend to be a philosophical treatise on epistemology or even what Hillman called an Epistrophe: a reversion, a return of phenomena to their archetypal and mythical background.[1]

Re-Vision's attention to craft rather than theory might imply an allegiance to Daedalus, the constructor of the labyrinth in which dark secrets could be hidden, or to Philyra, goddess of craft and healing who was full of shame at the birth of her son Chiron, the wounded healer, in half horse form. These myths may give a clue to the exploration – that like much therapy it will necessarily include the failure of the conscious ego to know or understand and a falling into a disturbing unknowing that may give birth to an unexpected healing. In keeping with the soulmaking method outlined in Chapter 5, we will follow the line of what has emerged through the Re-Vision training as necessary to engage the mysterious and often confusing work of psychotherapy.

Working with a supervisee recently, it became clear that she wanted help with a disturbance that had erupted in a supervision group of hers. Rather than help her to sort this out, it seemed important to me to positively connote the disturbance as a necessary part of the supervision and therapeutic process. It is uncomfortable to be disturbed, especially if you have a professional role for which people are paying and have expectations towards you. Along with this highlighting of disturbance have come two stories that offer their own disconcerting effect on any nice clean lines I might try and draw about psychotherapeutic knowledge and knowing.

- In a court in Alaska where local Yup'ik fishermen are on trial for flouting a ban on fishing king salmon, the jour-

nalist contrasts the evidence of biologists with indigenous locals 'speaking of how the salmon's spirits would
be offended if they did not show up to catch them'.[2]

- Kohn, in his fascinating book on 'How Forests Think',
  gives the example of indigenous people recognizing why
  their dogs were barking to illustrate the problem of 'oth-
  erness'. He states, 'human-to-human intersubjectivity
  and even trans-species sympathy and communication
  are not categorically different'.[3] The evidence he cites is
  that the Runa believe that their dogs dream and interpret their barks. This is in stark contrast to what we
  might think of as evidence and – if forests think – a challenge to our ideas of what is animate.

It seems to me that these two examples offer something of the
radical approach to knowing what the 'Impossible Profession' requires.[4] Although we may be schooled in reflexive practice, to
wonder about what it is that makes it possible for us to do this
work when its nature is so uncertain requires a different order of
exploration – perhaps more of a reverie or dream than a conceptual analysis. A reverie would at least be congruent with the
method. We get a hint from Hillman who points out in *Dream
and the Underworld* that since Freud named dreams as the royal
road to the unconscious, there has been a one-way street full of
morning (post dream) traffic moving out of the unconscious toward the ego's city.[5] He says he wants to face the other way to
move into the dark. So I hope not to stray too much into the light
in this exploration.

What has emerged in this integrative training was never a consciously schemed or logically planned development. It was more a
case of kinships with difference or affinities that were reciprocated
based on experience rather than concepts and theories within the
different modalities that members of the training came with. In
the exchange of experience based on different methodologies and
different ideas, there were certain affinities that emerged out of an
inter-experience. As Ronnie Laing wrote in 1967:

I cannot experience your experience. You cannot experience my experience. We are both invisible men. All men
are invisible to one another. Experience used to be called
The Soul. Experience as invisibility of man to man is at the
same time more evident than anything. *Only* experience
is evident. Experience is the *only* evidence. Psychology is
the logos of experience. Psychology is the structure of the
evidence, and hence psychology is the science of sciences.[6]

Direct evidence is hard to come by. Traditional Zen and Taoist
masters might instruct a student to know a tree through becoming
the tree but such unmediated knowing takes discipline. David
Abram draws on Merleau-Ponty's work in the *Phenomenology of
Perception*[7] to suggest that the distancing and objectification of
others comes through reflecting, whereas experience itself is revealed through the life-world – the implicit, primordial world we
take for granted.[8] Merleau-Ponty utilizes words such as intermingling and chiasm to reach for this reciprocal affinity between per-
ceiver and perceived. The epistemology of western science has
been based on divorce from experience in order to objectively perceive the data. I shall be exploring a different kind of knowing in
this chapter that is congruent with a relational modality of psychotherapy and an experiential learning methodology.

Experience as evidence can be complex, as Laing points out,
but it is a good starting point for a psychotherapy that is based on
craft and a learning model of *inside-out learning*. It means that we
give attention to the phenomenology of the event – even though
how you describe this through your perception, imagination,
memory and language will differ from my description. Something
of what you say may illuminate something from my experience
which I had missed or overlooked. And just this enquiry into our
difference makes for a template of psychotherapeutic enquiry. Or
we could say with the Laing quote above that the 'logos of experience' is knowing the difference and that is equivalent to Bateson's
much quoted statement that 'information is the difference'.[9]

In the interchange of experience, I don't start from the superior
place of the knower who can overrule or explain your perceptual

memory or imaginative fantasies. Nor do I assume, as it is your experience that you are describing, that this is sacrosanct and cannot be questioned. Along with many humanistic modalities, I respect your experience and recognize that I cannot know it. The story you tell me about your experience is what can be explored and there can be a tension between your story and how I have construed it and my experience of your telling. The enquiry is into the difference of experience between us – the *inter-experience*. Another way of talking about inter-experience is that it is relational.

The rather slow turn in psychoanalytic thinking through the inter-subjective, which Laing explored half a century ago, to the relational is very welcome.[10] One of the points of difference between some of these relational theorists and the epistemology worked with in this chapter is how that mutual connection comes about. The notion of an *interactive field* seems to imply that the connection comes about through the inter-action of the participants. This notion presupposes a causal relationship in which the participants are primary and their connection is a result. In contrast, our postulation of how we come together is that our relationship is already implicated before the meeting. The relation is primary. As we come together, this implicate relational field becomes explicit but we did not cause it. It showed itself through us. It is that 'third entity', explored further in Chapter 3 on the Third Body.

This 'third' is completely different to scientific ideas about the third world being objective knowledge. Since the critique of the postmodern, claims of objectivity have been deconstructed to reveal their cultural relativity. We see the first type of knowing as that of subjective experience, which as Laing points out is invisible to others – and may even be hidden from myself. The second is the conceptual knowledge about things, which is what passes for knowledge in most of our educational systems. The third is an inter-subjective or relational knowing that is constellated through inter-experience. It is the status of this third kind of knowing that I shall be exploring and attempting to show that this type of knowing fits the logos of psyche. It fits first because it is not borrowed from another domain such as physics but is intrinsic to the psyche, and second because, as Laing says above, 'Psychology is the logos of experience'.

The strange thing about this 'Third' is that, while it remains unthought, it is often overlooked and agency is assumed to be with the participants. Not wanting to entertain Donald Rumsfeld's 'pondering on unknowns', we give more attention to the implicit assumptions that lead to assuming agency as individual. This is both a philosophical and cultural problem that is not fitting to a relational universe in which we recognize that everything is connected to everything else. There could be a number of culprits for this overemphasis on the individual, including the misunderstanding of the Jungian notion of 'individuation'. We posit a version of the 'hero myth' as a key cultural complex that still draws people into its powerful grip.

The myth of the solar hero is prevalent in many civilizations going back into antiquity and featuring in modern myths such as that of *Star Wars*. Like the sun that rises each morning, the hero may suffer but will rise again. As Joseph Campbell's seminal work, *The Hero with a Thousand Faces*, shows, the hero personifies the culture's quest for identity in his or her capacity to overcome dangers and triumphantly return to the community with gifts.[11] Our modern western culture has been caught in the Prometheus version of this myth, in which stealing fire from the gods has allowed us such technological progress that we no longer need the favours of these gods. As such, the gods have transmogrified into the glamour of celebrity culture or possibly inhabit such celebrities that exercise a mythic grip on our media.

From the viewpoint of the soul, what we need today are lunar heroines, rather than solar heroes, who are willing to undertake a harrowing journey of descent into the 'Underworld'. They understand that re-vitalizing comes from that deep source within the collective psyche. The challenge of descent, so foreign to the upward ambitions of the solar hero, is a humbling stripping away of pretensions and an opening of the channels to sorrow and grief. The gift that returns with them is that of profound acceptance of interdependence and with it a new way of perceiving. Not only are we not at the centre of everything but we are also participants in a co-evolving world.

Laura Sewall, in *The Skills of Ecological Perception*, suggests that an

> ... inclusive, relational view of the world differs in appearance from one consisting of quantified, utilitarian objects. If we legitimize and practice a relational view, we act in response to a world that reveals forces and vibrancy, one that appears dynamic, and by extension, alive. This practice allows for our own engagement. We may find ourselves being "part of," or "in relationship with".[12]

Taking this paradigm shift to being 'part of' and 'in relationship with' other humans and the other-than-human world, we may wake out of our techno-dream, a nightmare of being the very alien from which we were trying to escape, and enter an animate world in which everything is speaking to us. David Abram, among others, has sought to free us from the dissociated but intoxicating complex of reflective abstract thinking in which we have become trapped.[13] It is as if we have extracted the animate magic of the earthy world, leaving it dry and arid, to become entranced with the magic of the two-dimensional screen in which letters have no relationship with the sensual world.

A major task of psychotherapy could be to repair this rupture with the world through offering to re-imagine and to re-story our relationship with it. Given our slow awakening to the climate crisis in which we exploit the world as 'other' than ourselves, so that we are left feeling like visitors who live on the planet rather than inhabitants who live within it, this would be a timely cultural intervention. It also widens the epistemological underpinnings of 'Relational Psychotherapy' to include all relationships – not solely the human-to-human ones.

Problems, as Bateson pointed out, do not arise within individuals but, through a network of relations, certain behaviours and beliefs establish themselves.[14] Psychotherapy, through limiting the networks to the human realm, leaves us with an impoverished epistemology. For instance, empathy is often defined as the ability to feel and share another person's emotions. We tend to only extend this to pets and herd animals such as horses, and only because they seem able to read us emotionally. It is difficult for us not to put humans at the centre of our epistemology. Not unlike previous paradigm changes, such as those of Darwin (no divine ancestry) and Freud (we are not in conscious control), the challenge is to decentre and see ourselves as participatory partners in complex systems rather than heroic masters.

Given this overall frame, the next part of this chapter seeks to pull together several important threads in the epistemological weave that Re-Vision has woven. These threads are a response to what we perceive as flawed logic in some traditions within psychotherapy. These include:

1   Normative thinking inevitably develops ideas of right/wrong and binary options.

2   Linear notions of development that operate from out dated Newtonian thought.

3   Idea of therapeutic objectivity belonging to a notion of nineteenth-century physics.

4   The split between inner and outer and psychotherapy's idealization of the 'inner' as exclusively addressed to human thought.

5   The belief that conceptual knowing is what supports therapists in their work.

6   Holding that abstract thought is superior, leading to an emphasis on theoretical exchange by therapists rather then engaging with our work as a craft of soulmaking.

Students in training are often looking to find out what is the right way of doing things. Their anxiety about getting it 'wrong' makes them look for answers. This has strong parallels with the therapeutic situation in which clients can look to the therapist, like to a doctor, to set them right. They are suffering in some way and want the psychological equivalent of pain relief. There are indeed times when the situation is straightforward and why not give the advice?

The important reluctance of therapists to do so comes from attempting to establish a form of relationship that is not that of a teacher who educates or of a doctor who asks what is wrong and prescribes a cure. There is also the danger of the split in the healing archetype in which the therapist seems to be cured and the client carries all the toxicity.[15] Despite an understanding of this danger, the temptation to be helpful and relieve the client is endemic and most clients come with this expectation.

The inside-out learning model refutes this 'helping frame' by insisting on the evidence base being the student's own experience. This requires trainers to deconstruct their 'expert teacher' frame and set up situations of mutual enquiry, which avoid the binary option of right/wrong, good/bad in favour of recognizing a diversity of responses that are more or less attuned to the nature of the enquiry. So yes there is something to be learnt but there is no universally correct answer, as every client system is different and unique.

A key aphorism at Re-Vision is, 'It is not wrong'. This does not imply that 'it' is right or that therapists do not make mistakes – only that a normative assumption of being wrong is misplaced. This is not an issue of ethical epistemology but a norm or critical injunction imported from family or subculture that carries with it questionable assumptions and values. The challenge to the 'wrong' judgement can subvert this limiting perception. The psychological work is in understanding why it might not be wrong. An enquiry into the client's story often reveals an old story or context for seeing and understanding that no longer fits the present experience. A simple example is that of a man complaining about a compulsion to cry at inconvenient moments. Having a stiff upper lip may have been an appropriate survival mechanism when younger but now creates relationship problems. Far from being 'wrong', the tears are a symptom of his relational and probably tender needs. Releasing this outdated context and its implicit values that make the symptom wrong, allows the symptom to be seen with new eyes and fresh meaning.

This applies as much to the therapist's intervention as it does to the trouble about which the client is complaining. The 'not-wrong' serves to inhibit reflex normative thinking and create that vital imaginative space to revision. For the therapist, the reasons why an intervention is not wrong tend to get explored in supervision where there is a reflexive distance within which the therapist can imaginatively wonder how the intervention fits or belongs in a wider context. In a recent supervision session, a supervisee was concerned about his sense of feeling out of his depth. When we attended to this as a counter-transference phenomenon, what emerged was a sense of awe. This was something he had not previously noticed. As in the previous example, far from being wrong (out of his depth), this was an opening to recognize that there was a need to work at a deeper, more soulful level.

This demonstrates how a different way of thinking and knowing can impact the practical craft of therapy. It is through the practice of inhibiting and deconstructing normative thinking that new imaginal ways of thinking and knowing can emerge. There is a skill in the craft that is a relational skill, concerned with attunement and being able to hold the uncertainty of not knowing. Keats recognized this is an essential aspect of the creative process and named it *negative capability*.[16] He was speaking of the capacity to resist premature closure in the creative process; to stay with the unfolding experience without reaching for some preconceived notion or theory as to what is unfolding. We can see that the 'not wrong' aphorism serves as an extension to negative capability through breaking open the binary system of right/wrong and facilitating a trust in the creative process.

In therapy, it is silence that often constellates this tension. The client may be struggling with the uncertainty inherent in therapeutic space that does not follow social patterns of civility. If it is the therapist's rule not to break this silence then the probability curve has collapsed and there is no tension to hold. The painful quality of the silence can become a kind of torture that lands solely with the client. If the therapist is engaged in a mutual exchange, then the tension, the possibly creative tension, is between them – an inter-experience. The enquiry can then be into what sort of silence it is. What does experience offer – or better, what does an imaginative exploration of experience offer? Is it a heavy silence like the heaviness of air before a thunderstorm? Is it a blue silence that comes from a melancholic depth? Is it a harsh silence that might break into an angry outburst? Through holding the tension, their encounter self-organizes. Through reading the implicit signs of their meeting, the silence becomes eloquent of meanings with which words might flounder.

Holding the tension also allows for a distillation of possible meanings. When there is no 'right' meaning everything has to be felt and attended to as a possibility. T. S. Eliot's phrase, 'Waiting without hope', belongs to this keening of the imagination, this negating capacity that inhibits the ready solution which the ego-mind proffers to escape the ordeal of the tension.[17] There is no straight line in this process. It is circular, a continual returning to the ever-present moment of the encounter. This recursive nature is represented in the Re-Vision Wheel, which recognizes that we meet the same type of 'trouble' at different levels within any therapist-client system.[18] This circularity reflects the relational knowing outlined above, in which everything is interconnected with everything else. It also reflects a soulful view of the psyche that understands that its depth is endless and there is always a deeper level of an experience that can be triggered or exposed as the couple system of therapist-client becomes ripe for this new emergence.

On the matter of the therapist's 'objectivity', the notion of a pure observer whose analysis has made them free of subjective response has been outmoded since counter transference was recognized as an essential aspect of the psychotherapy craft. We consider both that the therapist will be affected or even infected by what is displaced or projected out by the client and that the relational field will similarly be 'affected' by a therapist who is a participant in the mutual exploration. Rather than attempting the impossible task of being a pure observer, we see the craft as that of learning to monitor internal responses and images that occur as the therapist senses what is being displaced into the field through their own vulnerability. This looks similar to many relational analysts.

What perhaps accentuates this craft is the epistemological position that everything belongs to the system and is necessary to it.

So within the therapist/client system, to make a therapist's internal response 'wrong' or explain it personally – such as having left home in an irritated or sad state – would be to step outside the system. While the therapist-client system may utilize the therapist's previous state, it cannot be explained by it. The response necessarily belongs to the relationship. The enquiry becomes as to how it belongs, the meaning of how it fits, rather than explanations from outside the couple.

An exacerbating factor in this exploration of psychotherapy as the *logos of experience* is that of the unconscious. Whatever value this idea had originally in decentring humans from the ego's locus of control has been eroded through its becoming a concept and hence in the domain of the ego. It seems to have become a place within us in structural models of the psyche. Its place is to be the opposite of the conscious in another binary system along with day/night and shadow/light. It is seen as having no agency in itself, only through its affect on the conscious in terms of slips of the tongue, symptoms or complexes. It has become an explanatory concept for understanding processes that are not in the control of the rational ego. Hillman suggests that:

> It serves best the analytical mind, which works by taking and keeping things apart. What would analysis analyse were there no unconscious? How could it make conscious and how could we become conscious were there reservoirs of unconscious material requiring to these modern procedures of enlightenment?[19]

The notion that the unconscious is within us is part of the hegemony of the ego, which wants to rule through colonizing and ascribing everything unto itself. What if the unconscious is not within us? If anything we are like floating icebergs of ego within the sea of the unconscious. Even though this metaphor decentres us, it still functions as a topological view of the psyche. To stay with our focus on knowing through experience, what we need to inquire into is the nature of unconscious experience. Within the topological view of the psyche this is a contradiction in terms, for we need to be conscious to experience. The best we can hope for are fishing trips where we send lines down into the unconscious to see what we might pull up and even then there are problems of translation into language (interpretation). We cannot drag the underworld into the upper-world without loss.

This topological view of the psyche does not account for the manner in which 'the unconscious' seems to have agency and sometimes a deep knowing or wisdom. Clearly the type of knowing that is viable in depth psychotherapy is of a different kind than that of the world of the daylight ego. It is not even the implicit sort of knowing in which we know more than we can say, suggested by Polanyias as necessary for learning skills or remembering a melody.[20] Nor does it fit into the scheme proposed by Daniel Kahneman of two human operating systems: System 1 (intuitive, automatic, fast) and System 2 (more deliberate, more logical, slower).[21] It is this strange *knowing of a third kind* that involves some sort of experience that requires a poetic expression. It also requires containment for the inevitable anxiety involved in this exploration, especially with students who are often concerned with 'how to do it'.

The method is to journey down and enter this dark realm beyond the ego's rule. The process of entering into the other world is akin to an initiation into a new way of being that involves a frightening separation from the known. The process of descent may lead us to *suffer the meaning*. Not explain it with our rational ego but through the torment and grief intrinsic to the descent, we suffer and comprehend in totality.

To give an example from a seminar on narcissism, initially little account is taken of different theories. We start with an exploration of ways in which we feel special. This drops us into the field where issues of our worth, our difference and our gifts in the sense of what is precious to us, rub shoulders with feelings of shame, inferiority and wanting to compensate for that.

Later I read from the myth of Narcissus where he comes to the pool. Each participant imagines themselves at the side of a pool and looks through the surface deeply into its dark depth. Through having practised trusting the imaginal, most are engaged with an experience that touches deeply into their psyche. After a period of incubation they are invited to write a short poem that holds something of this experience. The reading out aloud of these poems is terrifying, exposing and remarkably transformatory. The poems vary from haiku, like ones such as:

> My hot tears fall
> In a cold pool

To the whimsical:

> If we two are truly one
> If we are by love entwined
> Then are you my slave
> Or am I yours?

The experience of seeing through the pool into its depth starts an imaginal journey through a liminal dreamscape. It requires a return journey that is facilitated here through a poetic expression. It is only later that a bridge is attempted to cognitive thinking and the process of translation of this deep experience into a common language of psychotherapy theory. While inevitably something is lost in this translation, the thinking is founded in the logos of experience and through the sharing of such experience, including of reading the poems, an *inter-experience*. This moving between different ways of knowing and being is a significant skill for psychotherapists to acquire and facilitates a trust in deep experience, not being just personal but belonging to an intersubjective knowing.

At Re-Vision the culmination of learning to work with this *knowing of a third kind* comes with the Research Seminars and the writing of a dissertation. It took many years to evolve a method of research that was congruent with our style of depth psychotherapy. It could not be one of the heroic ego's colonizing of new ground in triumph. The approach to knowing needs to find a way between pseudo objectivity and arbitrary relativism that draws on the intersubjective and stays close to experience as evidence, rather than reaching for the abstractions of conceptual knowing. Initially we settled on Transformational Research, as it recognized that the researcher was also in the frame and would him/herself be changed.

From a Transformational perspective, the subjective responses invoked in the researcher become part of the raw material of the study rather than something to be discarded or got rid of. This requires a high level of reflexive practice and a willingness to deconstruct one's perspective and be transparent – skills that are relevant to psychotherapeutic practice. Their inclusion in research belongs to the criteria of *relevance, authenticity* and *transparency* rather than those of generalizability, reliability and validity. The transformational method, rather than trying to eliminate the effects of the researcher, tries to understand and indeed celebrate them, and to make them clear to others.

Over recent years, there have been several new and exciting modes of research including heuristic, autoethnographic and hermeneutic research. With the publication of Romanyshyn's *The Wounded Researcher: Research with Soul in Mind*, we found a close match to our own work in that it gave precedence to the wound being the seed of the research.[22] It links the calling of the researcher with their own grief and wounding. It gives attention to both the ungrieved threads of the past and new emergent potential for what remains unsaid, untold – the soul of the work. It offers an epistemological strategy that allows the researcher to be consciously in the service of the work without being unconsciously identified with it. Since no rational language can express the fullness of psyche, the researcher must be content to signal the 'gap' between what can be written and what is.

The idea of this gap parallels the importance Re-Vision has given to the liminal space as a fertile void through which *knowing of a third kind* can emerge. Romanyshyn notes the difference between what has been said in the work and the soul of the work that remains unsaid. He recommends that we make a space, allow the gap, respect the fissure, welcome the abyss, and says:

> ... psychological language is a way of speaking into the gap between meaning and the absence of meaning, a way of speaking of meaning as a presence that is haunted by absence... In the gap and on the bridge across the gap between presence and absence, our words become an

elegy not only for what one must let go of, but also for what has been left behind or otherwise marginalised... which keep open a space for a return of what has been forgotten and is waiting to be remembered.[23]

His approach to re-searching and knowing he calls *Alchemical Hermeneutics*. This makes space for the unconscious process and so deepens the possibilities of knowing beyond that of the ego-mind. He writes, 'The wounded researcher is a complex witness who, by attending not only to the conscious but also to the unconscious subjective factors in his or her research, seeks to transform a wound into a work. The work comes through the wounding... '[24]

Another significant parallel to the approach outlined in this chapter is the relational knowing, in this case between the soul of the work that is calling the researcher and the ego of the researcher who is writing the dissertation. It becomes a reciprocal process in which the researcher has to sacrifice ownership and control of the work and become in service of the calling. The creative tension between these two allows poetics to become the voice of research that keeps soul in mind. It involves an imaginal indwelling, a metaphoric sensibility that attends to the images, fantasies, dreams and myths rather than concepts and facts. It is a circular journey to know what is already implicitly or unconsciously known.

An example from a recent graduate's abstract to her dissertation reads,

My re-search began with the experience of trauma activation in my body and the realization of the connection to and the impact of transgenerational trauma. My methodology has been to take the images that have come to me through the researching process and allow them to speak to this theme. In this process I explore: the impact of unprocessed transgenerational trauma on the undifferentiated experience of the baby; an archetypal frame that reveals the sacrifice of Eros in the refusal

of life that is suicide; the indigestibility of toxic unprocessed unconscious material and how this manifests in
the therapeutic relationship; the process of alchemical
digestion and the retrieval of the body; and finally the
honouring of the sacrifice and the surrendering of the attachment to what is toxic and the reclamation of Eros.
In following the images and listening to my body knowing, I discover an alchemical process of digestion that includes: a re-membering of what has been forgotten; a
retrieval of the body; an embodiment of the image; and
the transformation that can only come through a radical
surrendering of what has been lost. This surrender speaks
to me of a radical hospitality to the other that is both me
and not me, mine and not mine.

This exploration is underpinned by field theory; the
archetype of the wounded healer; Hillman's view of
pathology as messenger of soul; neuroscience and
trauma; and alchemy as metaphor for the process of individuation. All this is informed by and integrated into
the Re-Vision Wheel model.[25]

There are a number of points in this abstract that can be highlighted in terms of the approach to a *knowing of a third kind*. These
include:

- Allowing emergent images to speak to the theme of the
  research.

- An archetypal frame of the sacrifice of Eros in potential
  suicide.

- The indigestibility of toxic unprocessed unconscious
  material and alchemical digestion.

- This digestion that includes: a re-membering of what
  has been forgotten; a retrieval of the body; an embodiment of the image; and the transformation that can
  only come through a radical surrendering of what has
  been lost.

The cyclic nature of this exploration is also evident, if in an implicit way as befits an abstract, in the descent into transgenerational trauma and a healing reclamation through repeated cycles of mourning, remembering, and letting go. The external examiner commented on,

> ... its radical engagement with Hillman's exhortation to let the image speak, whilst, at the same time, informing and guiding the reader through a journey that necessitated surrendering to the process. The letting go of an 'egoic' need for structure and knowing is a huge challenge that has been well met.

Ending Reflection

There is at the end the sense of so much unsaid, that inevitable gap between the inspiration and what my language can hold. As with the nature of a circular or spiral epistemology the process of knowing or re-searching has no arbitrary closure but continues. This has parallels with the writing of a dissertation that must be handed in while the searching continues its recursive journey.

There is perhaps one absence whose magical presence is seldom sufficiently acknowledged – that is Hermes. While attempts are made to draw on his name with travel and communication companies, his trickster magic has made it hard for him to be pinned down. Yet his stealthy movements between the worlds as a guide to souls, and his ambiguous revealing/hiding powers could make him a personification of this third kind of knowing. In contrast to a Promethean demand for power and control, his hermeneutics keep open potential meaning. He offers a reclaiming of a participatory kind of knowing where the subject/object divide and the knower's alienation from knowing dissolves and allows a new sense of belonging.

What I hope has emerged in this chapter is both the many threads on which the Re-Vision approach has drawn and also its unique configuration or weave of these threads into a viable cloak for therapists to wear in their challenging work and play with the mysterious nature of psyche. The hermeneutic cloak of knowing in a third way is both transparent, so as to reveal rather than hide the therapist's vulnerabilities, but also containing, so that it holds us as we explore the logos of experience that is soulmaking.

[1] James Hillman, *Dream and the Underworld* (New York: HarperCollins, 1979).

[2] Adam Weymouth, 'Kings of the wild frontier', *The Sunday Essay, The Observer* (13 May 2018), at https://www.theguardian.com/commentisfree/2018/may/13/sunday-essay-kings-of-wild-frontier-salmon-run-alaska (accessed 18 July 2018).

[3] Eduardo Kohn, *How Forests Think: Toward an Anthropology beyond the Human* (London: UCLA Press, 2018), p. 86.

[4] Janet Malcolm, *Psychoanalysis: the impossible profession* (London: Granta Books, 2012).

[5] James Hillman, *Dream and the Underworld* (New York: HarperCollins, 1979).

[6] Ronald David Laing, *The Politics of Experience* (London: Penguin, 1967), p. 16.

[7] Maurice Merleau-Ponty, *Phenomenology of Perception* (London: Routledge, 1965).

[8] David Abram, *The Spell of the Sensuous* (New York: Vintage, 1996).

[9] Gregory Bateson, *Steps to an Ecology of Mind* (New York: Ballantine, 1972).

[10] Ronald Laing, H. Phillipson, and A. Russell Lee, *Interpersonal Perception: A Theory and a Method of Research* (London: Tavistock Publications, 1966).

[11] Joseph Campbell, *The Hero with a Thousand Faces* (Princeton, NJ: Princeton University Press, 1972).

[12] Linda Sewall, 'The Skill of Ecological Perception', in Theodore Roszak, Mary E. Gomes, and Allen D. Kanner, eds, *Ecopsychology: Restoring the earth, healing the mind* (Berkeley, CA: Counterpoint, 1995), p. 209.

[13] Sewall, 'The Skill of Ecological Perception'.

[14] Bateson, *Steps to an Ecology of Mind*.

[15] Both the problem of an enquiry as to what is wrong and this split are described more fully in Chapter 5, 'Soul and Soul Making'.

[16] Stephen Hebron, 'John Keats and 'negative capability'', *Discovering Literature: Romantics and Victorians*, The British Library website (15 May 2014), at https://www.bl.uk/romantics-and-victorians/articles/john-keats-and-negative-capability (accessed 18 July 2018).

[17] Thomas Eliot, *Four Quartets* (London: Faber, 1944).

[18] See Chapter 1, 'Roots and Seeds', in this volume, Figure 1.2.

[19] James Hillman, *The Myth of Analysis* (Evanston, IL: Northwestern University Press, 1977), p. 173.

[20] Michael Polanyi, *The Tacit Dimension* (Chicago, IL: University of Chicago Press, 2009).

[21] Daniel Kahneman, *Thinking Fast and Slow* (London: Penguin, 2012).

[22] Robert Romanyshyn, *The Wounded Researcher: Research with Soul in Mind* (New Orleans, LA: 2007), p. 194.

[23] Romanyshyn, *The Wounded Researcher*, p. 29.

[24] Romanyshyn, *The Wounded Researcher*, p. 111.

[25] Used with the author's permission.

Last Words

Our theme on the soulmaking craft of psychotherapy is not easy to convey in words. Many writers have commented on the challenge of translation and its inevitable losses. There is an impossibility of ever truly transferring what is in the oral tradition and a deeply experiential process into something that is fixed, separated out from the flow of lived experience, and captured. As Beckett says, 'Every word is like an unnecessary stain on silence and nothingness'.[1] (But, of course, even Beckett has to use some words to communicate the superfluousness of words!)

In the varied case descriptions in this book are common threads in the craft of soulful therapy: the tolerating of uncertainty, the holding of suffering, and the pathos. This pathos includes collective distress as well as individual wounds and vitalizes the therapeutic field to bring out some delightful synchronicities – a marker of Hermetic magic. Here, we hope that the words have caught at least some of the quicksilver in the craft. They speak of the emergent underworld as *mycorrhizal* – full of the unseen interconnected threads that give rise to a resonant field and synchronicity.

Despite talk of a hermeneutic method, Hermes has mostly remained invisible in this book. He slides out of view when anyone tries to pin him down. He hangs out on the borders and in the in-between, liminal twilight that has also been a central theme of the contributors. In contrast to a culture obsessed with celebrity limelight, Hermes keeps his magic in the margins, hidden in the half-light. Yet his presence is there in the gap between the words.

The divergence in method and craft described in the chapters is striking. Difference in a complex system, such as a training organization, is a mark of potential creativity as it signifies tolerance of 'deviance' and acceptance of new possibilities. Ensuring that shadow is given a place in this training means that windows are created through which the 'unthinkable' can be seen and named. Along with acceptance of difference, this speaks to an integration that weaves different ideas together into a practical therapeutic craft – a living practice that continues to develop from its dreamt origins.

While the style of depth psychotherapy at Re-Vision may be counter-cultural in a time of commodification and instrumentalization, there is also a growing recognition that what counts as evidence in randomized controlled trials may be trivial in terms of any sustainable transformation, and even questionable in terms of better social adjustment. True depth is not easily reached. It takes persistence and courage to transform woundedness into soulmaking. It requires a digestion of what has previously been felt to be poisonous, foreign and other. Journeys to Hades are not to be found in glossy tourist magazines, especially when they take five years of intense exploration, as the Re-Vision training does.

Although such transformational journeys are made individually, the claim in this book is that they are also cultural catalysts for a collective change – a radical re-visioning of our world view – one that will involve humbling challenges to a narcissistically wounded culture that so desperately wants to be seen as special, and which defends itself through increasing dissociation so as not to face into painful realities. Therapy can collude with this need to be special and with the cultural value given to individuality. Conversely, it can be integral to the process of de-centring ourselves from feeling we are the apex of everything. Learning to share in the delights and challenges of living on this planet together with other species – that is the vital human task we need to undertake in these troubled times.

Chris Robertson & Sarah Van Gogh
September 2018

[1] 'Samuel Beckett Talks About Beckett', Interview with John Gruen, *Vogue Magazine* (December 1960), p. 210.

Bibliography

Abram, David. *Spell of the Sensuous*. New York: Vintage, 1996.

Aron, Lewis. 'Analytic impasse and the third: Clinical implications of intersubjectivity theory', *International Journal of Psychoanalysis* 87, no. 2 (2006).

Assagioli, Roberto. *Psychosynthesis: A Collection of Basic Writings*. Wellingborough: Turnstone Books, 1965.

Avens, Robert. 'Imagination is Reality'. In *Western Nirvana in Jung, Hillman, Barfield and Cassirer*. Thompson, CT: Spring Publications, 1983.

Balint, Michael. *The Basic Fault*. London: Tavistock Publications Ltd., 1968.

Barfield, Owen. *Saving the Appearances*. New York: Harcourt Brace, 1957.

Barks, Coleman. *Rumi: Selected Poems*. London: Penguin Books Ltd., 1999.

Bateson, Gregory. *Steps to an Ecology of Mind*. Chicago, IL, and London: The University of Chicago Press, 1972.

Beebe, Beatrice, and Frank Lachmann. *Infant Research and Adult Treatment: Co-constructing Interactions*. Hillsdale, NJ: Analytic Press, 2002.

Beisser, Arnold. *The Paradoxical Theory of Change*. www.Gestalt.org (1970).

Benjamin, Jessica. 'Beyond Doer and Done To: An Intersubjective View Of Thirdness', *Psychoanalytic Quarterly* 73 (2004).

Benjamin, Jessica. *Beyond Doer and Done To: Recognition Theory, Intersubjectivity and the Third*. London and New York: Routledge, 2018.

Bernstein, Jerome S. *Living in the Borderland: The Evolution of consciousness and the challenge of healing trauma*. London and New York: Routledge, 2005.

Berry, Thomas. *The Great Work: Our Way into the Future*. New York: Bell Tower, 1999.

Bion, Wilfred R. *Experience in Groups*. London: Tavistock, 1959.

Bion, Wilfred R. *Second Thoughts: Selected Papers on Psycho-Analysis*. New York: Jason Aronson, 1967.

Blake, William. *Songs of Innocence and Experience*. Oxford: Oxford University Press, 1970. Poem first published in 1789.

Blake, William. *The Marriage of Heaven and Hell: Illuminated Manuscript with Original Illustrations by William Blake*. Oxford University Press, 1975.

Bly, Robert. *Loving a Woman in Two Worlds*. London: Harper & Row, 1985.

Bohm, David. *Wholeness and the Implicate Order*. London and New York: Routledge, 1995.

Breslauer, S. D. *Martin Buber on Myth – An introduction*. London and New York: Routledge, Taylor & Francis Group, 2015.

Buber, Martin. *Between Man and Man*. New York: Macmillan, 1965.

Buber, Martin. Cited in Richard Hycner. *Between Person and Person: Toward a Dialogical Psychotherapy*. Highland, NY: The Gestalt Journal Press, 1993.

Buber, Martin. *I and Thou*. Translated by Walter Kaufman. New York: Touchstone, 1996.

Buzzell, Linda, and Craig Chalquist, eds. *Ecotherapy with nature in Mind*. San Francisco: Sierra Club Books, 2009.

Campbell, Joseph. *The Hero with a Thousand Faces*. Princeton, NJ: Princeton University Press, 1972.

Campbell, Joseph, and Bill Moyers. *The Power of Myth*. London, New York: Doubleday, 1986.

Cozolino, Louis. *The Neuroscience of Human Relationships: Attachment and the Developing Brain*. New York: W. W. Norton & Company, Inc., 2006.

Dickinson, Emily. *A Choice of Emily Dickinson's Verse*. Edited by Ted Hughes. London: Faber and Faber Ltd., 1968.

Donleavy, Pamela. *Analysis and Erotic Energies in The Interactive Field in Analysis*. Edited by Murray Stein. Wilmette, IL: Chiron, 1995.

Eliot, T. S. *Four Quartets: The Dry Salvages*. London: Faber & Faber Ltd., 1944.

Fox, Matthew. *A spirituality Named Compassion: Uniting Mystical Awareness with Social Justice*. Rochester, VT: Inner Traditions, 1999.

Frankel, Richard. *The Adolescent Psyche*. London and New York: Routledge, 1998.

Freshwater, Dawn, and Chris Robertson. *Emotions and Needs*. Buckingham: Open University Press, 1980, 2002.

Freud, Sigmund. 'The Unconscious'. In *Standard Edition* 12. London: Hogarth Press, 1915.

Gerson, B. *The Therapist as a Person*. Hillside, NJ: Analytic Press, 1996.

Gibson, James William. *A Reenchanted World*. New York: Metropolitan Books, 2009.

Guggenbuhl-Craig, Adolf. *Power in the Helping Professions*. Thompson, CT: Spring Publications, 1983.

Hafiz. *The Gift: Poems by Hafiz*. Translated by Daniel Ladinsky. New York and London: Penguin Compass, 1999.

Hakim, Jami. *Yusuf and Zulaikha*. Translated by David Pendlebury. London: Octagon Press, 1980.

Hartley, Linda, ed. *Contemporary Body Psychotherapy: The Chiron Approach*. London: Routledge, 2009

Haule, John Ryan. *The Love Cure. Therapy Erotic and Sexual*. Woodstock, CT: Spring Publications, 1996.

Hayes, Jill. *Soul and Spirit in Dance Movement Psychotherapy*. London: Jessica Kingsley, 2013.

Heidegger, Martin. *Being and Time*. Oxford and Cambridge, MA: Blackwell Publishing Ltd, 1962.

Hillman, James. *Dream and the Underworld*. New York: HarperCollins, 1979.

Hillman, James. *Healing Fiction*. Thompson, CT: Spring Publications, 1983, 1994.

Hillman, James. *Insearch: psychology and Religion*. Irving, TX: Spring Publications, 1979.

Hillman, James. *Inter views*. Thompson, CT: Spring Publications, 1983, 1991.

Hillman, James. *Puer Papers*. Dallas, TX: Spring Publications, 1979.

Hillman, James. *Re-Visioning Psychology*. Oxford: Harper Perennial, 1975, 1977, 1992, 1998.

Hillman, James. *Suicide and the Soul*. Thompson, CT: Spring Publications, 1978.

Hillman, James. *The Essential James Hillman. A Blue Fire*. Edited by Thomas Moore. London: Routledge, 1990.

Hillman, James. *The Myth Of Analysis: Three Essays in Archetypal Psychology*. Evanston, IL: Northwestern University Press, 1972.

Hillman, James. *The Soul's Code: In Search Of Character And Calling*. New York: Random House, 1996.

Hillman, James. *The Thought of the Heart and the Soul of the World*. Thompson, CT: Spring Publications, 1992.

Hillman, James. *We've Had a Hundred Years of Psychotherapy – And the World's Getting Worse*. New York: HarperCollins, 1992.

Hirons, Tom. *Sometimes a Wild God*. London: Hedgespoken Press, 2015.

Hori, Victor Sogen, Richard P. Hayes, and James Mark Shields. *Teaching Buddhism in the West; from the Wheel to the Web*. London: RoutledgeCurzon, 2002.

Houston, Jean. *Myths for the Future*. Sounds True Incorporated, 1995.

Hycner, Richard. *Between Person and Person: Toward a Dialogical Psychotherapy*. Highland, NY: The Gestalt Journal Press, 1993.

Ingold, Tim. *On Being Alive*. London: Routledge, 2012.

Jung, Carl G. *C G Jung. Letters. Vol 2, 1951 -1961*. Edited by Gerhard Adler. Hove: Routledge, 1976.

Jung, Carl G. *Modern Man in Search of a Soul*. London: Routledge, 1933.

Jung, Carl G. *Psychology and Alchemy, The Collected Works*, Vol. 12. New York: Princeton, 1953.

Jung, Carl G. *The Practice of Psychotherapy, Collected Works*, Vol. 16, 2nd edn. London: Routledge & Kegan Paul, 1966.

Jung, Carl G. *The Psychology of the Transference, Collected Works*, Vol. 16, 3rd edn. Princeton, NJ: Princeton University Press, 1974.

Jung, Carl G. *The Red Book: Liber Novus Philemon*. Edited by Sonu Shamdasani. New York: Norton, 2009.

Jung, Carl G. *The Structure and Dynamics of the Psyche*. London: Routledge, 1960.

Jung, Carl G. *Two Essays on Analytical Psychology*. New York: Dodd, Mead & Co, 1928.

Kahneman, Daniel. *Thinking Fast and Slow*. London: Penguin, 2012.

Kalsched, Donald. *The Inner World of Trauma: Archetypal Defenses of the Personal Spirit*. London: Routledge, 1996.

Kerenyi, Karl, and James Hillman. *Oedipal Variations: Studies in Literature and Psychoanalysis*. Woodstock, CT: Spring Publications, 1991.

Kohn, Eduardo. *How Forests Think: Toward an Anthropology beyond the Human*. London: UCLA Press, 2018.

Laing, Ronald David. *The Politics of Experience*. London: Penguin, 1967.

Laing, Ronald David, H. Phillipson, and A. Russell Lee. *Interpersonal Perception: A Theory and a Method of Research*. London: Tavistock Publications, 1966.

Lawrence, D. H. *The Complete Poems of D.H. Lawrence*. New York: Viking Press, 1971.

Levertov, Denise. *Poems 1960 – 1967*. New York: New Directions Books, 1983.

Levine, Peter. *In an Unspoken Voice: How the Body Releases Trauma and Restores Goodness*. Berkeley, CA: North Atlantic Books, 2010.

Macy, Joanna. *World as Lover, World as Self: Courage for Global Justice and Ecological Renewal*. Berkeley, CA: Parallax, 1991

Malcolm, Janet. *Psychoanalysis: the impossible profession*. London: Granta Books, 2012.

Merleau-Ponty, Maurice. *The Phenomenology of Perception*. London: Routledge & Kegan Paul, 1962, 1965.

Mitchell, Stephen. *Influence and Autonomy in Psychoanalysis*. Hillsdale, NJ: Analytic Press, 1997.

Mitchell, Stephen. *Relationality: From Attachment to Intersubjectivity*. Hillsdale, NJ: Analytic Press, 2000.

Moore, Thomas. *Care of the Soul; A Guide for Cultivating Depth and Sacredness in Everyday Life*. New York: Harper Collins, 1992, 1994

Moore, Thomas. *Sex and the Soul*. New York: Harper Collins, 1998.

Murdock, Maureen. *The Heroine's Journey: Woman's Quest For Wholeness*. Boston, MA: Shambhala, 1990.

Music, Graham. *The Good Life: Wellbeing And The New Science Of Altruism, Selfishness And Immorality*. London and New York: Routledge, 2014.

Neumann, Erich. *Amor and Psyche: The Psychic Development of the Feminine: A Commentary on the Tale by Apuleius*. Princeton, NJ: Princeton University Press, 1956.

Nietzsche, Friedrich. *Beyond Good and Evil*. New York: Vintage Books, 1989.

Odgers, Andrew, ed. *From Broken Attachments to Earned Security: the role of empathy in therapeutic change*. Abingdon, Oxon and New York, NY: Routledge, 2004.

O'Donohue, John. *Beauty*. London: Harper Collins, 2004.

Ogden, Thomas H. 'On potential space', *International Journal of Psychoanalysis* 66 (1985).

Ogden, Thomas H. 'The Analytic Third: Working with Intersubjective Clinical Facts', *International Journal of Psychoanalysis* 75 (1994).

Paley Ellison, Koshin, and Matt Weingast, eds. *Awake at the Bedside: Contemplative Teaching on Palliative and End of Life Care*. Somerville, MA: Wisdom Publications, 2016.

Perera, Sylvia Brinton. *Descent to the Goddess: A Way Of Initiation For Women*. Toronto: Inner City Books, 1981.

Plotkin, William. *Soulcraft. Crossing into the Mysteries of Nature and Psyche*. Novato, CA: New World Library, 2003.

Polanyi, Michael. *The Tacit Dimension*. Chicago, IL: University of Chicago Press, 2009.

Pullman, Philip. *His Dark Materials*. London: Yearling, 2001.

Rilke, Rainer Maria. *Book of Hours: Love Poems to God*. New York: Riverhead Books US, 1997.

Robertson, Chris. 'Dysfunction in Training Organisations'. *Self & Society* 21, Issue 4 (1993).

Robertson, Chris. 'Hungry Ghosts: Psychotherapy, control and the winds of homecoming', *Self & Society* 41, Issue 4 (2014).

Rohr, Richard. *Immortal Diamond: The Search for our True Self*. London: Society for Promoting Christian Knowledge, 2013.

Romanyshyn, Robert. *The Wounded Researcher: Research with Soul in Mind*. New Orleans, LA: Spring Publications, 2007, 2013.

Rosen, David. *Transforming Depression*. York Beach, ME: Nicolas-Hays, 2002.

Roszak, Theodore, Mary E. Gomes, and Allen D. Kanner, eds. *Ecopsychology*. San Francisco, CA: Sierra Club Books, 1995.

Russell, Dick. *The Life and Ideas of James Hillman, Vol 1: The Making of a Psychologist*. New York: Helios Press, 2013.

Rust, Mary-Jayne. 'Climate on the couch: unconscious processes in relation to the environmental crisis', *Psychotherapy and Politics International* 6, no. 3 (2008).

Rust, Mary-Jayne, and Nick Totton, eds. *Vital Signs*. London: Karnac, 2012.

Sands, Susan. 'Self Psychology and Projective Identification', *Psychoanalytic Dialogues* 7 (1997).

Schaverien, Joy. *Desire and the Female Therapist*. London: Routledge, 1995.

Schore, Allan. *Affect Regulation and Repair of the Self*. New York and London: Norton, 2003.

Schwartz-Salant, Nathan. *The Mystery of Human Relationship: Alchemy and the Transformation of the Self*. London: Routledge, 1998.

Schwartz-Salant, Nathan, and Murray Stein. *Archetypal Processes in Psychotherapy*. Wilmette, IL: Chiron Publications, 1987.

Searles, Harold. *The Nonhuman Environment In Normal Development and in Schizophrenia*. New York: International Universities Press, 1960.

Sedgewick, David. *The Wounded Healer: Countertransference from a Jungian Perspective*. London: Routledge, 1994.

Sharp, Daryl. *The Secret Raven: conflict and transformation in the life of Franz Kafka*. Toronto: Inner City, 1980.

Shengold, Leonard. *Soul Murder*. New York: Ballantine Books, 1990.

Sherman, Josepha. *Mythology for Storytellers*. London: Routledge, 2015.

Shorter, Bani. *An Image Darkly Forming; Women And Initiation*. London and New York: Routledge, 1987.

Sommer Anderson, Frances, ed. *Bodies in Treatment: The Unspoken Dimension*. New York and London: Analytic Press, 2008.

Stein, Murray, ed. *The Interactive Field in Analysis*. Wilmette, IL: Chiron Publications, 1995.

Stern, Daniel. *The Interpersonal World of the Infant*. London and New York: Routledge, Taylor Francis Group, 2018.

Stolorow, Robert D., and George E. Atwood. *Contexts of Being: The Intersubjective Foundations of Psychological Life*. New York and Oxford: Routledge, Taylor and Francis Group, 2002.

Stolorow, Robert D., and George E. Atwood. 'The Intersubjective Perspective', *Psychoanalytic Review* 83 (1996).

Totton, Nick. *Embodied Relating*. London: Karnac, 2015.

Totton, Nick. *Wild Therapy: Undomesticating inner and outer worlds*. Ross-on-Wye: PCCS Books, 2011.

Turner, Victor. 'Betwixt-and-Between: The Liminal Period in Rites de Passage'. In *The Forest of Symbols: Aspects of Ndembu Ritual*. Ithaca, NY: Cornell University Press, 1967.

Turner, Victor. *The Forest of Symbols: Aspects of Ndembu Ritual*. New York: Cornell University Press, 1967.

Van der Post, Laurens. *The Heart of the Hunter*. UK: Vintage Classics, 1968.

Van Gennep, Arnold. *The Rites of Passage: Anthropology and Ethnography*. London and Henley: Routledge & Kegan Paul, 1960.

Watzlawick, Paul. Change: *Principles of Problem Formation and Problem Resolution*. New York: Norton, 1974.

Weber, Andreas. *Matter & Desire: An Erotic Ecology*. White River Junction, VT: Chelsea Green Publishing, 2017.

Weil, Simone. *Gravity and Grace*. Translated by Emma Crawford. London: Routledge, 1947.

Weller, Francis. *The Wild Edge of Sorrow: Rituals of Renewal and the Sacred Work of Grief*. Berkeley, CA: North Atlantic Books, 2015.

Welwood, John. *Towards a Psychology of Awakening: Buddhism, Psychotherapy and the Path of Personal and Spiritual Transformation*. Boston, MA: Shambhala, 2002.

Whitmont, Edward. *Return of the Goddess*. New York: Crossroads, 1982.

Wilber, Ken. 'The Pre/Trans Fallacy', *ReVision* 3, no. 2 (Fall 1980).

Wilber, Ken. *Up From Eden: A Transpersonal View of Human Evolution*. Abingdon: Routledge & Kegan Paul, 1981.

Winnicott, Donald. 'Further thoughts on babies as persons'. In *The Child and the Outside World: Studies in developing relationships*. Edited by J. Hardenberg. London: Tavistock Publications Ltd., 1957.

Winnicott, Donald. *Playing and Reality*. New York: Tavistock Publications, Routledge, 1971, 1991.

Winnicott, Donald. *The Maturational Processes and the Facilitating Environment*. London: Routledge, 1965; Abingdon and New York: Karnac, 1990.

Winnicott, Donald. 'Transitional Objects and Transitional Phenomena A Study of the First Not-Me Possession', *International Journal of Psychoanalysis* 34 (1953).

Woodman, Marion. *Addiction to Perfection: The Still Unravished Bride*. Toronto: Inner City Books, 1982.

Wordsworth, William. 'Intimations of Immortality from Recollections of Early Childhood'. In *The Penguin Book of English Romantic Verse*. Edited by D. Wright. London: Penguin Books, 1968. Poem first published in 1888.

Wordsworth, William. *Poems 1815*. General Books LLC, 2009.

Yalom, Irving. *Love's Executioner and Other Tales of Psychotherapy*. New York: Basic Books, 2012.

Yeats, William Butler. 'The Second Coming'. In *Selected Poetry*. Edited by A. Norman Jeffares. London: Macmillan, 1962.

Biographies

Contributors

Joan Crawford BA, MSc, is a UKCP registered psychotherapist and also trained as a dramatherapist. She has a private practice with both clients and supervisees. Her background includes broadcasting, running a fringe theatre, and living in a meditation centre. She completed her psychotherapy training at Re-Vision. Her current interest is in Ecopsychology and the ways in which the wider context of planetary crisis may be impacting clients. She is a facilitator of Be The Change Symposium, addressing issues of environmental sustainability, social justice and spiritual fulfilment. She is a member of the Ridhwan School of spiritual development.

Nicky Marshall is a UKCP registered psychotherapist and recognized training supervisor, as well as a BACP accredited senior practitioner. She is qualified in Couple Counselling and Supervision, and holds the European Certificate of Psychotherapy. She has been a trainer for nearly 20 years. She has a particular interest in relationship dynamics, our relationship with the other than human world, and the ethics of practice, and has published on the subject of the transpersonal ethics of supervision. She has a background in Mental Health, working with addictions and with survivors of sexual abuse in childhood. She is currently the Director of Training at Re-Vision.

Chris Robertson BSc, MPhil, has been a psychotherapist and trainer since 1978. He studied meditation in India, humanistic group work, child psychotherapy, psychosynthesis and family therapy. He co-founded Re-Vision in 1988 from which he is now retired. Since 2018, he has been the chair of the Climate Psychology Alliance. He contributed the chapter 'Dangerous Margins' to the anthology *Vital Signs* (Karnac, 2012); is co-author of *Emotions* and *Needs* (OUP, 2002); and authored several articles including 'Hungry Ghosts: Psychotherapy, control and the winds of home-coming' (Self & Society 2014). He co-edited the *Psychotherapist* (2016: 63) on *Climate Change, Despair and Radical Hope.*

Ewa Robertson MSc, MBPsS, is a UKCP registered psychotherapist, trainer and supervisor with 35 years clinical experience. In 1988 she co-founded Re-Vision in London, which runs integrative and transpersonal Counselling and Psychotherapy diploma trainings. She also teaches at other psychotherapy training centres. She has become increasingly interested in the relationship between psyche and soma. Her approach to psychotherapy is based on and influenced by relational and body psychotherapy, attachment theory, developmental psychology, neuroscience, and post-Jungian analytical and archetypal psychology. She is trained in somatic trauma therapy.

Jo-Ann Roden BSc (hons), is a Re-Vision-trained, UKCP-accredited psychotherapist currently working in private practice as a psychotherapist and supervisor and at Re-Vision in a tutor/trainer role. Jo-Ann gained much of her early clinical experience working as a therapist in a young persons substance misuse service, holding a particular interest and focus on the Hidden Harm agenda. Jo-Ann continues to be engaged, therapeutically, by the long-term impact of early childhood trauma and neglect on the development of the self.

Mary Smail is a Dramatherapist (Sesame) trainer and psychotherapist (Re-Vision) working in private practice. She teaches *Stories of Soul Making* to Re-Vision psychotherapy students. Mary's work began using the folk arts in Christian liturgy. She then directed the Sesame Institute charity from 2006 to 2015. She is co-author of *Dramatherapy with Myth and Fairytale* and runs *Psyche and Soma*, a course which offers health professionals the opportunity to apply embodied imagination and soulmaking in their practice. She has published several chapters on creativity and soul, the most recent being 'Open Sesame and the Soul Cave', in the *Routledge International Handbook of Dramatherapy.*

Sarah Van Gogh has worked as a counsellor in private practice since 2001, and is on the training staff at Re-Vision. She was a counsellor and a trainer for many years at Survivors UK, the London charity that supports men who have experienced sexual abuse. Before training as a counsellor, Sarah gained a degree in English from Cambridge University, and then worked in the fields of theatre, community health and adult education. She has written about the connection between therapy and the expressive arts in a number of journals, and is the author of *Helping Male Survivors of Sexual Violation to Recover*, published by Jessica Kingsley.

Artists

Una d'Aragona holds a first class fine art degree from University College Falmouth Cornwall. She exhibits regularly in Cornwall, London and Bath, has been selected for numerous exhibitions and won the Amiri South West Award at the National Open Art Competition.

Julie Harding is a UKCP registered psychotherapist and an artist. Her works are both figurative and abstract, often drawing on inspiration from nature, exploring space, form and colour. In recent years her work is a process driven or emotional response to the inner landscape and the psychotherapy process and she is particularly drawn to the art of alchemy. She uses acrylics, oils, collage and mixed media.

Also available

Transpersonal Dynamics offers approaches to the therapeutic encounter from the leading edge of quantum physics field theory and integrative psychology.

Transpersonal Dynamics is the culmination of over 20 years of feedback about 'what works', gathered through delivering integrative and transpersonal training to counsellors, coaches, psychologists and psychotherapists who work with organisations, adults, couples, families, young people and children.

Using down-to-earth language in a practical way, this book addresses some of the gritty aspects of the therapeutic relationship, with the aim to inspire and support practitioners to take more risks to bring a collaborative, relational quality to their work.

Stacey Millichamp is a trainer on the Masters Degree in Psychotherapy and the Diploma in Integrative and Transpersonal Clinical Supervision at the Psychosynthesis Trust *in London, and teaches on the Diploma in Supervision with Soul at the* Re-Vision Centre for Integrative Psychosynthesis *in London. She is the Director of* Entrust Associates, *which provides counselling to staff and students of secondary and primary schools in London.*

isbn 978-1-912-618-00-4 (print) / 978-1-912618-00-1 (ebook)

TransPersonal
Press

Lightning Source UK Ltd.
Milton Keynes UK
UKHW022200020720
365920UK00005B/745